RED IN THE CENTRE

*The Australian bush
through urban eyes*

MONTE DWYER

Monyer Pty Ltd

Red in the Centre
published by
Monyer Pty Ltd
Ph 0412 422 699
Email info@monte.com.au

This edition published 2012
Reprinted 2013, 2018
Copyright © Monte Dwyer 2008

The moral rights of the authors have been asserted.

ISBN: 978-0-646-49296-4

Printed in Australia by McPherson's Printing Group, Maryborough, Victoria

10 9 8 7 6 5 4 3

To my father Russell
for all the laughs

THANKS

To Macquarie Southern Cross Media for the job; to Charlie and the rest of the *Across Australia* crew for making it easy; to RV Asia–Pacific for the Hymer; to Tim Fischer for his support; to my readers James Mansfield, Iain Riggs, Gavan Curry, Bernie Dwyer, Kevin and Anna Anderson, Kym Crosbie and especially Terry Dwyer, Ross Gallen and Clive Dorman for helping me shape the ill-defined early drafts into a more readable offering; to Kerry Davies for the polishing touches; and to Julieann Brooker and Emma Sutton for the cover art and design.

And, finally but most importantly, thanks to the many Australians who generously contributed to this book. I chose to leave you with your anonymity (wherever possible) because I know what a precious thing that is, and because I wanted the integrity of each exchange to shine brighter than its gossip value. On occasion I have also taken small liberties with the content of our meetings – for the sake of clarity, brevity, and levity – but I have tried to remain true to their essence. As far as I'm concerned the trip was bejewelled by every last thoughtful, curious, struggling, clever, sad, ambitious, warm, nutty, generous-spirited, amusing, loud, lonely, lost and found one of you, and I wouldn't be trapped on this big desert island with anyone else.

Cheers
Monte

FOREWORD

In 1892, J. F. Archibald, editor of the *Bulletin*, which in those days was known as 'the bushman's bible', sent the disputative writer and poet Henry Lawson to the bush in order to save him from the ruinous temptations of certain seedy Sydney bars.

When your money is low, and your luck has gone down,
There's no place so lone as the streets of a town;
There's nothing but worry and dread and unrest,
So we'll over the ranges and into the West.

I am no Archibald, nor is Monte Dwyer, talented though he is, another bibulous Lawson but I thought of them both when a hundred and fifteen years later I sent our Mont 'up the country'. Of course I romanticise a little, but Monte was in 'Dwyer' need of a change. He is a clever, talented, likeable but rambunctious character, just like Henry. I thought he needed a patron. As Archibald was to Lawson, so I would be (or so I fancied) to Monte; I would encourage the incipient journalist inside the former TV weatherman. I would give him a climate change. I would be a patron, a patient guide, an indulgent parent to his creative *enfant terrible*.

There was a quid pro quo to my generosity. I needed a reporter, a man of the people, a wandering minstrel for my national radio program. A man who could travel what I call 'the heartland' and from out there, where the land meets the horizon, mine the yarns, muster the characters and harvest the flavours of Australia. I knew Monte could do the job and he knew it too. When I delicately proposed this employment he trampled me underfoot to leap aboard and take messy possession of the luxurious home on wheels, which inadvertently he would attempt to wreck over the next year or so.

Monte's travels more than satisfied the Archibald in me. He did a wonderful job sending back stories and interviews for my radio program such as we rarely hear now because, in our urban obsession, we have forgotten where we came from. When Lawson was out there, Australia's was a rural population. Two-thirds of us lived in the bush, in country towns, rural hamlets and lonely farmsteads. A hundred years later we are the most urbanised people on Earth, two-thirds of us now living in a handful of coastal cities.

Monte's radio reports and now this book of his adventures under the biggest skies in the world serve to remind us that an Australia without the bush is but a pale Californian shadow of what we should be. His stories remind us that the intrinsic Australian values – mateship, perseverance, self-reliance, loyalty, community spirit and ironic humour – were all hammered out on the harsh anvil of the bush.

Like Henry under the direction of Archibald, Monte has brought back his swag of stories now printed for the amusement and the instruction of Australians everywhere. In the bush these are times of dramatic challenges, which recall much of the worst that Lawson saw. These are times to test human hearts and to break the fiercest spirits. Monte has come back from what turned out to be his own life-changing pilgrimage with a book that will help Australia to better understand itself.

I am grateful to have played the smallest role in getting this tale told.

Charles Wooley

CONTENTS

CONTENTS

PREFACE

When I first told my father I'd been invited by the Prime Minister to attend the 2020 Summit he said, 'What on earth does he want you for?' Naturally, I told him the PM wanted my help running the country.

'God help us,' was all he said.

Similarly, my friends were undecided whether they should congratulate me or be afraid. I argued that I must be due congratulations, if only because I'd managed to convince the organisers I was one of Australia's 'best and brightest', when all evidence would suggest nothing could be further from the truth. They could not but agree.

The real reason I was selected to attend was because I was the nominated media representative for Charles Wooley's radio program,* for which I'd just spent the previous year travelling the country, sourcing and broadcasting stories from regional Australia.

I'd landed the radio job after I'd called Charlie to scrounge some publicity for a book I was trying to flog at the time, called *Slapped by an Angel*. Charlie had countered with an offer to help with publicity, providing, he said, 'I jumped in a campervan and ventured out where the horizon meets the sky to find stories from the heartland.'

So, from drought to flooding rains, through changing seasons and federal governments, I figure-eighted the country (and many an ill-shaped detour besides) talking to people about life in the bush. And, one by one, the people I encountered opened up my narrow, city-centric view and provided me with a fascinating portrait of what's really going on in this country's 'heartland' at present.

It is this portrait I attempt to paint for you here, and also this portrait I armed myself with before the 'best and brightest' at the Summit; but more on that later. For now, enjoy the trip.

* *Across Australia*, broadcast on the Macquarie Southern Cross Media network.

DÉJÀ VU

I've done this drive before: Cobar to Wilcannia in the rain. The last time was thirty years ago with my father, after we'd just spent a couple of days on the Macquarie Marshes. The rain was so heavy we had to stop on the side of the road till the storm passed. Western New South Wales was lovely and green then.

We'd been exploring the Marshes in an inflatable rubber dinghy, checking out the birdlife – we were both avid birdies – but there was so much water about the mosquitoes were unbearable. So we had to camp up in dry country about five kilometres away. On the first morning the old man inflated the dinghy with a spark plug hose, and then put it on the roof of the Peugeot, which had no roof racks.

'Now you get in the thing while I drive up to the water,' said the old man.

'You're kidding.'

'No, it'll be all right. Your weight'll hold it down.'

'What if it blows off with me in it?'

'Don't be stupid: it won't come off. I'll drive slowly.'

'Haven't we got a rope?'

'Won't need to tie it down. Trust me, Son. I'll drive slowly.'

So off we set, the old man driving the Peugeot station wagon, me sitting in the dinghy on the roof, holding it down. But I doubt we travelled five hundred metres before he started accelerating, and I knew he'd forgotten I was there. My screams – and I hollered – were washing away in the wind-stream, he was picking up speed and there was absolutely nothing I could do but hang on till take-off and pray for a safe landing.

It would have made a great scene for a movie:

A dusty road in the Australian bush. A fluorescent orange rubber dinghy with terrified dork-pilot sailing off the top of a speeding white car, miraculously landing intact and right-

side-up about a hundred metres into the scrub.

Follow white car as it carries on past the dinghy.

Cut to a close-up of the man driving along, totally oblivious to the mayhem he's just authored, singing to himself.

Cut to dork-pilot climbing out of landed dinghy, shaken but unhurt, his gaze following the receding car.

Cut to the car pulling up beside a wide expanse of water. Man gets out looking satisfied as he surveys the scene: dead trees and lush reed beds punctuate the water, which stretches to the horizon, abundant birdlife wherever you look. Perhaps he follows the path of a startled cormorant, its wingtips kissing the water as it takes off. Then he remembers his cargo and notices it's missing.

Cut to a close-up of the man's face (as I remember my old man's face looking so many times when I was growing up)*: surprised and bewildered that such a thing could have happened to him, then concerned as he gets back in the car and turns it around.*

I know the Marshes will be a different story today. I can see they've had a little recent rain because there's green pick along the roadside, and the rain is still falling lightly as I drive. But I sense there'll be big changes ahead.

Wilcannia is a quiet little town on the Darling River, a significant part of the most important river system in Australia, the Murray–Darling. Normally you can sit under the old river gums and watch the water flow by. Today there is no river, not even a chain of ponds; just a few stagnant puddles and a water tank, which I'm told some of the local kids pushed in. When the river's up they jump off the bridge into the water, when it's down they roll around the riverbed in empty water tanks; that's when they're not substance-abusing or entertaining themselves with less innocent activities like stealing cars, damaging property, or worse – not uncommon pursuits for many rural Aboriginal kids with nothing better to do in twenty-first-century Australia.

I set up camp on the banks of the riverbed. This is the first time I've plugged the campervan into 240-volt mains power and I'm interested to see how it performs. I even get the fold-up table happening and put the awning up to make a real camp of it. I feel like an old hand.

In the morning the old hand drives off and leaves the 240-volt power cable hanging from its pole in the caravan park.

SLAPPED BY A PARROT

The first time I set eyes on the Hymer was at the official launch at the Sydney Caravan and Camping Show. Both Charlie and I had been flown in for the occasion and the motoring media was well represented.

At that stage the signage had not yet been applied, and my first impressions were of a modest-looking grey campervan with sleek contours and plenty of room inside. There seemed to be ample cupboard space, I liked the fact that each of the front seats could swivel around to make up six places at the dining table, and, though a bit on the pokey side, I was impressed by the shower and toilet ensemble. I'd never had a car with a bathroom before.

Someone also explained the lightweight aluminium-plywood body panels, but the advantage of saving about a tonne in body weight was lost on me at that stage. I would learn the significance of that feature later on.

It had a double bed with one corner cut off that the makers called a French bed (don't ask me), which lifted to allow access to the storage hold (clever), an open-plan kitchen with a gas cook-top (highly functional), a fridge (manual locking only, which is not enough for absent-minded novices: we need automatic locking to avoid regular spillage), self-locking drawers (that's more like it), and the dining table compressed down to make a base for the spare bed.

As far as the running gear went (that's what we industry types call the drivable section), the Hymer was matched with a Mercedes diesel Sprinter 316 CDI, which has more than enough power for such a light rig, and effectively meant the thing was capable of going like the clappers.

All in all it looked a very respectable unit, and I was just imagining myself climbing into the driver's seat and getting it out onto the roads less travelled when one of the motoring journalists sidled up to me.

'Do they know you've got form with motor vehicles, Monte?'

'You're kidding me. That was ten years ago.'

'Gone but not forgotten.'

He was referring to a brand new Range Rover that met an inglorious end while on loan to me for a trip to Cape York. To paraphrase from a letter the boss of Rover Australia sent the boss of my television network:

I recently lent the Today Show *a couple of vehicles in good faith, for use in the making of television for your network. One vehicle was returned to me looking like it had played host to every conceivable human activity barring ritual disembowelment, while the other I was forced to retrieve on the back of a truck …*

I wasn't very popular there for a while. And I wasn't even driving the one we threw away: mine was party central, which I'm almost positive never hosted a disembowelment.

'Are you sure you pair weren't buggering around? Racing, perhaps?' said my network boss with a look that really said, 'Think very carefully before you admit to anything of the sort.' (Only his terminology was considerably more colourful than that.)

'No, sir,' said my cameraman. 'We drove responsibly. The accident was … an accident.'

I thought the 'sir' a nice touch, and the accident qualifier pure genius.

'And what about you, Monte? You're not known for your tempering influence on people.'

While I wasn't impressed by the character assessment I thought it wise not to quibble, and blurted something about being the epitome of responsibility.

'The car rolled five times and ended up two hundred metres into the scrub! How is that responsible driving?'

Neither of us felt we had a satisfactory answer to that question, so we passed. The end result was the network provided Rover Australia with commercial air time equivalent to the value of the lost vehicle, and spared us our jobs. Just.

Anyway, apparently when they import a new model for advance publicity, every motoring hack in the country has to line up for a turn to review the thing. So, by taking the only two vehicles in the country out of circulation, we made quite an impact. At least according to the guy in my ear at the launch we did. I left him looking at the Hymer with a mixture of respect and pity, as if he believed he was seeing it for the last time.

The next time I saw the Hymer was post-signage, and this time my initial impression was of a highly immodest-looking campervan so loudly decorated it reminded me of a parrot. I'd expected something slightly less than subtle, given the design was conceived by commercial radio people, but even I wasn't prepared for the impact.

Essentially, staring out from each side of the van was a 2 x 2-metre portrait of Charlie, photoshopped over a mega-Australiana background complete with Uluru, kangaroo and sky of blue. (Sorry, got on a bit of a rhyming roll there.) Underneath Charlie's mug in blaring *look at me I'm a moron* font were the words 'The Hymer Happy Tramper'. And adding to this bizarre spectacle was the provocative little *Slapped by an Angel* cover perched up in the top corner, which looked a bit like a tart caught in the spotlights at church.

When I drove it home to load up for the trip the normally plentiful and vociferous wildlife in my street was shocked: noisy miners hushed, rainbow lorikeets paled, and the old lady up the street took one look and said, 'You'll never get lost in that.' It was an eleven out of ten.

That was when I decided to call it *The Parrot*.

DELIVERANCE COUNTRY

My itinerary has Toowoomba as the starting point, but I'm heading for Millmerran, about an hour or two further west, because I have a crazy cousin living there. His name is Dan the Man, or at least that's what we've called him since he was six months old. I have a photo of us when we were about three years old, and he's wearing one of those ridiculous bib-and-brace suits mothers insist on dressing their baby boys in that always make the child look like Chubby Checker. In his suit, Dan looks like Al Capone.

We're actually double first cousins, since our mothers are sisters, and our fathers are twins. This means we are genetically very close, and the likelihood of a successful organ transplant between us is high. I've been trying to talk him into swapping livers for years, but he doesn't think mine will fit inside his torso.

He has a goat farm in The Holdings to the west of town. The Holdings consist of maybe a hundred 25-acre lots, thirty or so 250-acre lots, and just enough nutters per capita to make the place truly interesting. Dan has two of the larger blocks side by side, and since he is a bona fide hillbilly he fits in perfectly.

When I say he has a goat farm, I mean he has goats, and he has a farm, but therein the similarities end. Since he let them loose on their own 250-acre paddock they haven't been sighted. He believes they're breeding up nicely and his herd is now almost double its original size, which will surely prove profitable when they finally eat everything in their holding and give themselves up in exchange for a feed. Meantime, the herd exists primarily as potential in Dan's mind, and in the very occasional distant bleating that only Dan's ears ever hear. As music, I've no doubt. It's just like virtual farming on the net only with less chance of selling the stock.

Before we arrived at his holding, Dan gives me the whistle-stop tour of the area. As well as virtual goat farming Dan works on a cotton farm, so we go to visit his boss. Unfortunately, we arrive at the same time as news of a tragedy does: a young girl on an interstate property has died as a result of being crushed in some cotton-picking machinery. That news haunts me for days.

We drive around and Dan points out the struggling sorghum crops and the cotton fields filled with suck holes made by the plants greedy for moisture. These were the first real signs I'd seen of the drought and, to state the obvious, seeing the crops dying in the fields made the issue more real than watching it on television.

Dan's wife is a strong woman with a salty beauty, who crinkles her nose like a schoolgirl when she laughs. She works at the local piggery and tells a yarn about coming home from work, stripping out of her stinking clothes in readiness for a shower, and getting sprung by an unexpected visitor. It's such an outrageous contrast between the image of a naked woman and the smell of pigs that I don't know whether to laugh or cough.*

That night we eat, drink and make merry till it's time for bed, and Dan walks me to *The Parrot* and leaves us alone for our first night together. It's a shaky start to the romance on account of having no power or shower – Dan has no 15-amp socket, and I've inadvertently tripped a valve release on the hot-water system and can't find it in the dark – so I go to bed dirty and sleep like the king of tramps.

The next morning we share a cuppa then go our separate ways: Dan to the cotton farm, his wife to the piggery, and me to my first full day of the trip.

The Parrot and I have begun.

* Later in the trip I would learn that piggeries were among the hardest hit by the drought, with the rising cost of grain and the increased competition introduced by the Howard government's Free Trade Agreement sending many to the wall, but at that stage I didn't know enough to even ask the questions.

A SAD THING

A sad thing just happened in the country. A young woman was killed. She fell into a cotton-module builder and was crushed. They flew her to the big city hospital but it was no use. She died anyway. She was eighteen years old.

When cotton is picked it gets packed into large blocks ready for transport to the cotton gins where it's processed. These blocks are called modules, and so the machinery plant used to make them is called a module builder. It's a simple affair, consisting of a large, bottomless steel bin, not unlike a giant builder's waste bin only without a floor, and with an overhead press. When the cotton is tipped into the bin an operator works the controls of the press to tamp down the cotton until it's well compressed. Raw cotton is a springy material and the tamping requires persistence, with the operator manoeuvring the press backwards and forwards over the layers of cotton many times before the module is sufficiently compacted. When the module is built the bin is lifted off, leaving the module ready for loading onto a flatbed trailer, and the process is repeated.

The girl was standing on the side of the bin as the hopper was delivering its load – as the workers often do to watch that the cotton is distributed evenly – and she fell in, unnoticed. The hopper driver didn't see her because he was busy making sure his load went where the press operator was directing him, and the press operator didn't see her because he was too busy giving the hopper driver instructions before he started tamping down the new load.

It's hard to imagine what she thought when she fell. Perhaps she giggled as she landed softly in the cotton, unaware she hadn't been seen. Or maybe she was aware of the danger from the outset, and screamed. Either way, it's academic. At some point she would have known she was in trouble, her muffled screams for help no match for the din of heavy machinery, her struggling pointless against a medium whose very softness was drowning her. Then she would have felt the press.

How they discovered her doesn't even bear imagining.

Life hasn't been kind to farmers lately. The worst drought in living memory, country services dwindling, and growing public agitation over the use of our diminishing resources.

And cotton farmers have been right in the firing line, with many arguing that it's a crop that shouldn't be grown in this country because of its heavy reliance on irrigated water and its high use of chemicals. These are valid arguments. But so too is the argument that cotton is an opportunistic crop, planted and grown by irrigators only when market forces and water availability deem it the best choice. Which makes it more flexible and, in an oblique way, less of a burden in times of drought than permanent plantings, which need water to survive year in, year out, whether it's there or not.

Whatever your belief, it seems we are all becoming experts in crop selection, and conversations speckled with terms such as climate change, sustainable agriculture and biodiversity are now common around city cafés and dinner tables. And cotton is often painted black. It's easy to pass judgement on something we can't see, aren't intimate with.

Out here these issues are as real as sweat. As the cliché goes, they have faces. And right now some of these faces you'd scarcely be able to look at, let alone confront with your ideas on how they should be managing our land.

The parents of the girl who died would have had their share of struggles in the past. Life has a habit of dealing them out just to keep you honest, especially life in the bush. But whatever came along they still had each other, and their kids, to keep them strong. Now where are they expected to draw their strength from? What keeps you going when you have to bury one of your children? The cruellest card in the deck.

Did she have siblings? I don't know. I hope so, for the parents' sake. I could have followed the story up and gathered those details but I didn't have the stomach for it, couldn't face them. I felt for them, wanted to offer something, anything, to show I cared in my own unrelated way, but I couldn't have looked into those eyes.

Surely there would have been grandparents, and aunts, uncles, cousins and friends, all with a vested interest in the life of this girl, and all now carrying the weight as best they can, each in their own particular way. For that sort of grief is at once the most private and collective of agonies, as if being part of an exclusive club that expects of its members great personal sacrifice to join, yet guarantees all inductees a lifetime membership.

And there's another face best avoided: that of the young man who was operating the press. Can you imagine how many times he will go over what happened, trying to find a loophole, a single moment he might return to and change the outcome? If only. What if? He may not have raised her from a baby like her parents did, kissed her better when she hurt, taught her right from wrong, but along with the guilt he will now carry like an errant gene for the rest of his life, he too will feel gutted by the lost potential. Just like her parents, he had shared her hopes and dreams for the future. He did so because they were entwined with his. He was her boyfriend.

Yes, a sad thing has happened out here. A very sad thing.

BOOTS, BEES AND BOURKE

I do my first live cross to Charlie's radio show from Toowoomba and, to be frank, I have nothing to offer. Luckily the mayor is on hand to talk about the recent failed recycled water referendum – that recycled water was rejected in such a conservative town is not surprising; that it's taken so long to become a serious issue in this country is truly staggering – so the sum total of my contribution on that first day is to play telephone receptionist.

Getting to Bourke was always going to be a big ask in one day; now that I've left Toowoomba late morning, that's an even tougher call, and the boots don't help. Whatever possessed me to buy turn-down boots I have no idea. With the ankles down I look like a queer Robin Hood, and turned up it feels like my ankles are shackled. I need to swap them.

Since Toowoomba has no affiliated store I hit the road and get on the phone again. Thus begins an amusing and drawn-out process of tracking down the owner of a store I can't remember the name of and convincing him to participate in an exchange plan involving Australia Post, a sketchy itinerary and him choosing a new pair for me.

At the time of writing I haven't yet reached the agreed return destination, but my man assures me they are a fine style of boot and one he'd have no hesitation wearing himself, in a colour he describes as 'a sort of masculine greeny-greyish cream'. You can imagine I can hardly wait to see what turns up.

The rest of the day I spend driving. I like driving, and I especially like being halfway between somewhere and nowhere in particular, which is pretty much where I end up. Somehow, between Walgett and Brewarrina I find myself lost. (I've always liked the contradiction in that phrase.) The first inkling comes when the tar abruptly gives way to gravel, and the confirmation when the gravel gives way to something decidedly more inferior.

Now *The Parrot* probably isn't designed for off-road travel, but I have to say it handles the conditions like a trooper. Just occasionally, when I'm cornering a bit quicker than I should be, the van feels like it's losing its poise; but, all in all for such a high-bodied rig, it really does stick to the road. And fly, for that matter. This is my first indication of how light it really is.

By dusk I'm so far away from knowing where I am I've given up consulting the map, and somehow end up at a cattle feedlot. For the uninitiated, that's where they fatten beef on a mixture of grain and hay and what-have-you, calculated to ensure the cattle put on weight at an optimum rate. You could think of it as a health retreat for cattle, with an all-expenses-paid trip to the city as a prize for completing the course.

There are fifteen or twenty blokes working at the feedlot – agreement was never reached – and they have about four or five thousand head of cattle to tend. They've got inventive nicknames – Jitterbug, Zipper, Alcohol – and all the usual concerns of young men working away from women. On Friday nights they go to a watering hole up the road called The Pub in the Scrub, which sometimes attracts crowds of up to a couple of dozen blokes. I imagine it's a hoot. We share a beer, they point me in the right direction, and I leave them with a copy of *Slapped* as thanks. What they'll make of it is anyone's guess, but the cover illustration alone is enough to get a few of the boys excited.

I don't quite make it into Brewarrina that night, and sleep in a roadside camp on the banks of a creek without water.

The next morning I fill up with diesel at Bree, as the locals say, and meet three beekeepers. They tell me they're scouring the country for honey flow, or blossom about to flower, where they can truck in their hives to work the pollen. And they're onto a patch of Heather Bush, which they extoll the virtues of for some time. Apparently bees working Heather Bush get hot, literally and metaphorically.

'Put your hand in a hive and you'll feel the heat,' one of the guys says. 'Trust me.'

They also tell me Heather Bush makes them busier than other bees so you can move them onto blossom the others are too lazy to work. But when they start banging on about honey being the logical successor to antibiotics and the cure-all for every ailment known to man, I realise these guys aren't just apiarists, they're honey worshippers. Honey is their god, and I'm looking like a potential convert.

'It works like a poultice,' one of them is saying. 'In fact, if you covered yourself in honey every day you'd never get sick.'

'But you'd have a hell of a time getting dressed,' I say.

My frippery has put them off and they decide I'm not worthy. We bid each other congenial goodbyes and go our separate ways.

The town of Bourke has contributed plenty to the elusive Australian identity. It took its name from a governor called Bourke – and not from the explorer Burke because he didn't need it anymore after perishing in the scrub – but since then the town has lent its name to a whole swag of Australianisms. The most obvious being the expressions 'back o' Bourke', referring to where I spent half the previous day, and 'going Bourke-o', which is what happens when you spend too long out the back o' Bourke.

Iconic Australian writer Henry Lawson claimed you had to know Bourke before you could ever know Australia, although he had been sent out there to dry out by his editor and was likely prone to extravagant fancies. And Fred Hollows, the man so many underprivileged people owe their sight to, is buried there.

Unfortunately, Bourke's in strife. The drought has hit them hard. They haven't had a cotton crop for four years, the citrus and market garden crops are only just surviving, upstream irrigation development has them worried they won't see water even if they do get rain, and almost a quarter of the town's population has left to find work elsewhere.

What can I say? Go, visit. Have a beer for Henry. Drop in and tell Fred what you've seen – he'd like nothing more.

From Bourke I consider taking the river road to Wilcannia, but the grey sky convinces me otherwise. Any rain at all on that black dirt and you don't go anywhere.

It rains before I get to Cobar.

Note: At the 2020 Summit I meet another beekeeper who reliably informs me that bees pollinate two-thirds of all the food we eat.

ALL THE DUMB THINGS

I admit there were some troubles early on while I adjusted to life on the road; indeed, it felt like the next twenty-four hours of my life were spent lurching from one idiot manoeuvre to another.

To begin with, the first thing I did when I crossed the border into Victoria was stock up on fruit and vegetables. The Sunraysia region is known for its fine produce, and even if the welcome sight of a real river was more illusion than reality – the locks and weirs keep the levels up even if there's negligible flow – it was still seductive after two thousand kilometres of country so needy it sucked your mouth dry. So I bought the whole shop.

Then I found myself a secluded spot to free-camp right on the riverbank at Mildura. Normally this wouldn't be such a bad move – at that point the Murray is wide and lazy, the banks are lined with old eucalypts and dreamy willows, and paddle steamers drift on by – but an earlier oversight returned to haunt me.

Inexplicably, I woke up in the wee small hours thinking about the power cable. Had I unplugged it at Wilcannia? Or was I now just so accustomed to the drill that I'd simply forgotten that I had? Not likely. A quick check of the hold confirmed what you already know, and ruined the rest of my night's sleep. I've no doubt this was covered in Campervanning 101, but I wasn't there.

Hymer, I'm told, is a big name in Europe, but in this country it's virtually unknown and getting a replacement cable wasn't going to be easy. The plug on this cable was weird enough to make even a good technician scratch his head.

I tried to read to pass the hours till daylight but *The Parrot* overruled my intentions and turned out the light. It's a clever feature, no doubt, to have the computer shut down non-essential services to preserve enough charge to start the vehicle, but I assure you I didn't appreciate it at the time. I couldn't even light the gas to make coffee!

Eventually, the slowest dawn in the history of the world broke and I rang my support guy, who told me not to worry – I think his actual words were 'get a grip' – because I could get a replacement in Adelaide, a mere five hours' drive away.

Then, when I tried to retract the cabin steps to set off, they wouldn't respond because of the aforementioned power shut-down feature. Later I learned how to override the computer to remedy this, but for the moment I was snookered. I could hardly drive to Adelaide with the steps down: it would be carnage, like the Roman chariots mowing down the Christians with wheel blades.

Another call to my support guy yields another grovelling confession, and he tells me the simplest way to get some charge in the battery is to rev the shit out of it for a while. Or at least that's how I interpreted his instructions.

So, in the quiet of a Murray River morning on the Mildura side of the way, a man places a house brick on the accelerator of a campervan and sets it screaming at near maximum revs. Then he walks some distance away and turns to watch, as if he is no more than an innocent bystander, bemused by the spectacle of this loudly decorated vehicle now making an auditory pest of itself as well.

My next folly came when I crossed the border into South Australia, and all the fruit and vegies I stocked up on, thinking I'd be in Victoria for a while, I had to hand over to a grinning quarantine official. (I have no idea what's so funny about confiscating a man's roughage.)

The trip from Loxton to Murray Bridge was pleasant enough. Though I did get *The Parrot* bogged – not for the last time on the trip, I might add – in the soft sand at the roadside. Single rear wheels no doubt improve on-road performance, but they surely don't help in anything less than firm underfoot.

I also forgot – again, not for the last time, not by a long shot – to lock the fridge door, and a bit further up the road its contents ended up on the floor. You really do need a bit of an anal-retentive streak to avoid this sort of thing in campervans, and I have nothing of the sort. In the end I just stopped carrying high-risk articles like eggs, beetroot and soft leftovers, unless they were in moon-landing canisters.

Somehow I found the caravan supply shop and collected my replacement cable without further disaster, then set off for Mount Gambier. I was determined I'd turned the corner with *The Parrot*. No more stuff-ups. I'd served my apprenticeship and from now on, I told myself, I was going to cruise like a pro.

Within the hour of course I got myself nicked for cruising a little too enthusiastically – at Policeman's Point if you don't mind – and, you guessed it, it wasn't the last time. Those lightweight body panels really did suck you into trouble. Eventually I discovered how the cruise control worked, but not before my driving licence was almost pointless.

And there were other minor mishaps and personal effronteries to endure along the way – most of which could only be of interest to the avid nomadic lifestyler or career sadomasochist, so I won't share all the tiresome details with you – suffice to say it wasn't a seamless transition to the wandering way of life.

STUDIO DANGERS AND STRANGE RIVERLIFE

The good news is my boots were waiting for me when I arrived at Mount Gambier. The bad news is whatever drugs my man at the other end is taking are not good for his eyes. The boots are polar bear white, with a choice of either cream or green elastic straps that pass as laces. I should have twigged with the 'masculine' qualifier in his description.

Charlie was broadcasting the show live from 'The Mount' and they liked me to join him in the studio whenever the show came to the mainland. It was normally networked from Hobart.

Now, Charlie is a very political animal who loves the parry and thrust of that 'blood sport', as he calls it, whereas I know almost nothing about politics. The contrast would be fine if the bastard didn't have a frightening habit of asking for your opinion on air, about something you'd never given a moment's thought to.

He caught me off-guard several times through the trip; most notably with the news of the federal government's Intervention Program in Aboriginal communities in the Northern Territory, which I hadn't a clue about till he asked me to comment.

'You've spent time in the communities in the Territory, Monte. What do you think about what they've done?'

'What who've done, Charlie?' I said, knowing it wasn't the strongest opening move I could have made.

And I could tell he knew he'd found a bunny by the way he relished describing the key elements to me – Aboriginal welfare, alcohol-related violence, child sex abuse, army-led task force et al – any one of which would be enough to merit caution; all of them in the one sentence could only be a minefield.

So I opted for the most inane response I could muster,

remembering the story of a young Kylie Minogue, upon being asked what she thought of the injustices in South Africa, answering, with the very best of intentions, how dreadful it was the way they were killing all their elephants.

Somehow I got through the Mount Gambier show without drawing attention to my ignorance on almost all matters of import, and afterwards went for a drive to Nelson, just over the Victorian border on the eastern bank of the Glenelg River.

In a weird twist, the Glenelg was swollen, and for the same reason the other rivers have all been down: no rain. Here they need rain to flush open the mouth to the sea, which silts up with sand when left too long without a clean-out.

That night I camped next to a wharf on the riverbank, and in the morning I did some fishing from my 'front deck' as I watched the riverlife idle by. I say fishing but what I was really doing was feeding the plague of small bream in the shallows. I was fast losing interest when I was visited by two notable parties.

First was a family from Narre Warren, who I discovered standing on my wharf staring at some of the waterbirds on the river. Being something of a birdy myself I took the opportunity to show off.

'I think they're Musk Ducks,' I said.

'Indeed they are,' said the father of the group, without taking his eyes of the ducks, 'also known as Submarine Birds. And those over there with the white patches and dark heads are Chestnut Teals. Those ones there, not quite as dark: Grey Teals. And hear that call, over there somewhere? That's a Black Duck: similar in appearance to the Grey Teal only bigger.'

It's clear I'm outgunned and I ask what got him so interested in birds.

'Pressure cookers,' his grown son answered, while his mother and father nodded their agreement, smiling. They were on a culinary tour of the Australian ornithological landscape.

The second noteworthy party cruised up to the wharf in a runabout just as I was about to give the fishing away altogether. They were two men from Portland, pulling in to get some bait.

They were knockabout-looking blokes in every respect except one: they were wearing dresses and high heels.

I tried to ignore their obvious fashion oversight and told them of my problem with the bait pickers. They suggested I wouldn't lose so many baits if I cast my line out into the middle of the river where there were fewer fish.

I said that reminded me of the old story about Socrates finding Plato searching for his wallet under a streetlamp, even though he lost it further down the street where it was dark.

'I'm looking for it here rather than where I lost it,' he told the enquiring Socrates, 'because the light's better.'

The two fishermen from Portland listened politely, before one of them said: 'You're a very strange man.'

And with that, they both hiked up their dresses and walked up the hill to the bait shop.

SALT AND VINEGAR CHIPS

When the south-east corner of South Australia was first settled back in the 1800s, it was basically under water: not much more than a wasteland of marshes and swamps. So some bright spark decided that if they dug channels westward to the ocean they could drain the land and make it available for farming.

'And over many years, that happened,' one of the region's oldtimers tells me. 'And even today there's an extensive network of drainage channels – up to a hundred million dollars' worth – taking place in the upper south-east, to relieve not only the water, but the salinity within the water.

'Agriculture has benefited greatly,' he continues, 'with a great diversification of crops resulting. But there's one little problem – or it's a big problem now – where the government has offered huge tax incentives for the city investors to grow Blue Gum plantations.'

He believes the established Radiata Pine industry is an asset to the area because it thrives on the marginal, hillside country and the end product is used locally. But not so the Blue Gums, which prefer the premium farm land and are grown mainly for the Japanese chipping market.

Blue Gum plantations also need a lot of water to survive, and he tells me it's inevitable there'll be water problems arising.

'If the drainage channels don't work effectively – and we're now seeing the Blue Gums lowering the water table – we don't have salt removed out to sea, and we'll very soon have a salinity problem as well as a supply problem.

'Furthermore, you compare a thousand hectares of Blue Gum plantation on valuable land, with the same area given over to livestock and cropping. Now, while I haven't heard which is the more profitable, I do know that the profit from the Blue Gums – which is taken at twelve to fourteen years, when they mature – goes mostly back to the cities. Whereas the profit gained from agriculture stays mostly in the district.

'Some small towns have now closed because Blue Gums have moved in, and people – and good luck to them – are offered huge sums of money to sell up and leave their farms. So it's breaking up communities, which is not good.'

He's been a farmer in the area all his life, just like his father before him, and his son, who listens respectfully while his father talks. There's not much about the region's history he doesn't know, and he speaks in an almost continuous stream with great concentration, head bowed to the floor.

'But one thing that most people don't seem to realise,' he continues, 'is when the land was first settled, well over a hundred years ago, people were offered generous taxation concessions to clear the forests – that grew, I might add, after drainage. But now the taxation laws have done a complete reversal, and the same type of city investor is being offered very generous taxation concessions to clear the hundreds of thousands of kilometres of fencing, windmills, woolsheds and farmhouses, to replant back with trees. People are totally puzzled by that one.

'It all gets back to which is the most valuable to the community,' he concludes, 'hardwood trees, or agriculture. I think agriculture. But the city investors are more capable of getting the ears of the politicians, and the farming communities are missing out. And I think that's very sad, very unfortunate.'

Then he stops speaking, but remains focused on the floor for some time before he looks up at me. It's only then I realise that since the start of the interview, which has run for about ten minutes, I've not asked one question.

NEEDS KNOWS

I find it hard to drive through Griffith and not think of drugs. This harks back to the late 1970s when anti-drugs campaigner and local businessman Donald Mackay disappeared, believed murdered, after being named in court as a police informant in a large marijuana bust in the area.

These days the alleged mafia presence is not so prominent. Some say they're focusing their horticultural talents on making good Calabrian-style vino, if you believe there is such a thing. Others say they moved to North Queensland and carried on, business as usual. But unless you have a need to know what they're up to, it's probably best you don't.

It made good sense back then to use Griffith as a base for growing illegal crops, since it was a long way from anywhere conspicuous and had a permanent supply of water. This was largely thanks to an experiment begun in the early 1900s by a bloke called Samuel McCaughey. Sam decided the area was perfect for gravity-fed irrigation because the land was flat and the clay soil would minimise loss through seepage. He argued way back then that it was not gold or any other mineral resource that would prove Australia's most precious commodity, but water. So he set out to prove his theory by irrigating his North Yanco property to fruition. The government was impressed enough to pick up the ball and run with it, and the Murrumbidgee Irrigation Area was born.

Today there are four thousand kilometres of canals irrigating almost two hundred thousand hectares of land, forming the core of the MIA and greatly contributing to the overall status of the Riverina as the premier food producing region of New South Wales.

Turn off the tap and the MIA reverts to semi-arid desert country suitable only for dry land farming, Griffith and Leeton all but disappear, New South Wales goes hungry and Australia loses revenue and hard-earned presence in several important export markets.

I meet with a heavy-hitter in the water industry and he gives me my first insight into how complex the whole game really is.

Who gets water and who goes without is broadly determined by a state government hierarchy of entitlements, which puts domestic and stock needs at the top of the list, followed by environmental and then agricultural needs.* Then there are different grades of water allocations, different conversion rates of entitlements, and terms like capping and unbundling to further confuse. Again, unless you need to know, it's probably best you don't.

I ask him how much loss there is with the open irrigation channels.

'A lot less than you might imagine. Probably no more than 15 or 20 per cent evaporation and seepage together. But I concede some of the dry land areas are a bit of a worry. Some of that country doesn't seem suitable for flood irrigation.'

'Why doesn't the area convert to line irigation?'

'Cost, mainly; both set-up and energy costs. Right now it's all gravity fed here, so there's zero energy cost.'

'What about solar?'

'In an ideal world that's the way to go, but solar energy is still about three times the cost of coal power. So, until it becomes more competitive, either through market forces or government rebates, it's unrealistic to expect farmers to use it.'

I talk to a businessman in Leeton who tells me most retail operators are hanging on, but praying that the promising start to the season continues. And that's pretty much the story across the board: farmers are sewing on the strength of the bit of rain they've had, and all they need is some follow-up and they'll get through, at least for one more year. There's a cautious optimism about the place.**

And as I drive around I can't help wondering what they did with Donald Mackay. It can't be an easy thing to make a human body disappear without a trace – not without a little help from your friends. So presumably there are a number of people still living with that dark secret. But then again, it's not really something I need to know...

---

* Under the new National Water Plan, the states will transfer responsibility of the resource over to the federal government when the individual states' agreements expire.

** Their caution was well founded: there was no follow-up rain, either here or anywhere else in eastern Australia, where a promising start encouraged farmers to sow heavily.

SMALL DIVERSIONS

I have a mate who's been telling me about Grong Grong, Matong and Ganmain for so long I feel like I was born there, so I call in to ask his mother if she recognises me as one of her babies. She doesn't, but since it's Friday night she recommends I go to the Matong Pub and ask around.

It's wheat, sheep and cattle country in these parts, and the three towns were originally spaced so closely because they were built around the pick-up points for the wheat. Before the days of bulk storage, the farmers used to stack their full bags next to the railway line for collection – these days, the trains stop to load up at the silos – and the towns just grew around the most obvious focal points. I guess someone opened a pub for the thirsty farm workers, who probably figured they might as well live within staggering distance, and the rest would have been nothing more than a logical extension of a good idea.

At the pub, the talk is about rain, both the recent and the dose 'due Tuesday',* and about seeding, and fishing, and football, and other life matters of the bush. One joker amuses me with stories about how stupid sheep are, and concludes by assuring me one day butchers would get found out for selling sheep brains, because there's surely no such thing.

But the story I remember most clearly is the one told to me by my mate's brother, about a benevolent old landowner.

'It's a beautiful property he's got,' he tells me. 'Runs right along the river as far as you can think. And even through the hard times the old bloke used to keep a couple of gardeners going, and a yardy or two, as well as his farmhands. And he had this rabbiter on the payroll for fifteen years. Fifteen years. Started there almost before he had whiskers, got himself married and had a family half-grown in the time.'

He pauses to make sure I get the correct weight, before continuing.

'So one day the rabbiter comes up to the old bloke and says, "I think I've got all the rabbits, Boss."

'And the old bloke puts his arm around his rabbiter's shoulders and says, "I'll tell you when you've got all the rabbits, son."'

And as he finishes, my storyteller's face becomes the study of admiration for the landowner who'd no more see his workers starve than see his own family suffer the same fate.**

* As she is spoke.

** The landowner was none other than Hugh Mackay, inventor of the Sunshine Harvester and renowned industrialist, whose battle with the unions over the right to pay his workers according to merit became the watershed case for determining the 'basic wage' in this country.

STEERS, BEERS AND AUCTIONEERS

I know I'm in trouble the moment I see him. He is archetype *Drinkus Australis*. Small, alert, quick, and thirsty: the kind of bloke for whom enough is never enough, merely a convenient starting point. He is my designated guide for Wagga Wagga. It is through his eyes I will see the place. It's only midday on Saturday. The signs don't look good.

As well as being an A-grade drinker in peak condition, my guide is also a stock and station agent, a tireless charity worker, popular and gregarious, so he knows almost every human being within a hundred-kilometre radius. Between, around and through beers, he sets about introducing me to every last one. If I missed you, I'm sorry. If I met you and don't remember, I'm sorry. If I'm too sorry, I'm sorry.

Saturday afternoon in an Australian pub has a particular feel. It's hard to define, but it's a mixture of resurrection and potential, with a distinctly masculine feeling of calm before a change. It's about football and form guides and peace. It's about friendships forged over trips to the urinal, and sealing fresh bonds with a round of 'do you know So-and-so from Such-and-such?' And it's about beer, in middies, pots, schooners, pints, handles, ponies, cans and stubbies. But never jugs. Because, most of all, Saturday afternoon drinking is about pacing yourself.

Somewhere along the line I forget what day it is. I remember being bear-hugged by King Crushawhiteboy, the Maori warrior who had evidently forgotten what year it was, never mind day. I remember having a punt on a horse called Pavlova because the publican pointed out how it had been scratched from Sydney in favour of a start in Melbourne over a shorter distance carrying less weight. I remember thinking he was a genius for noticing that, then changing my mind when the thing ran second last. And I vaguely remember being involved in a late night Calcutta auction and thinking I should never be given a microphone when I'm in that condition. I don't remember getting back to *The Parrot*.

Sunday is a much gentler affair and by mid-afternoon I'm feeling fit enough for a bit of a tour with my guide. He's visiting a client who has some sheep he wants assessed for sale. The sheep all look the same to me until the differences are pointed out.

'See those over there?' my guide says. 'A bit taller, longer in the face, they're Border Leicesters. And the smaller, neater-looking ones are Dorsets. The supermarket chains prefer the Dorsets because the legs dress down to the right size for the Sunday roast.'

Once I know what I'm looking for it's easy. The Dorsets are the pretty ones, and the Border Leicesters are the horse-headed plain Janes; with apologies to breeders who will no doubt disagree.

We visit another client at the saleyards. He's as old and bent as a river gum and still looks about as strong. His eyes have seen plenty, and they're weepy and red-rimmed.

My guide introduces us and I say, 'It's good to meet you.'

'It's good to be met,' he says, paying more than just lip service to the claim.

He's a cattle dealer who buys from all over and sells through the auctions for a margin. Today he's got mostly 'fats', or cattle to be sold for fattening up on the feedlots or that rare commodity in these times, a property with grass to spare. He also points out a Hereford bull 'killer'.

'Really?' I say. 'A killer?'

But he just smiles and shakes his head a little, not dismissively, rather to give me a chance to get it for myself. I do. A killer isn't the crazed bovine murderer my imagination had determined, but a beast on its way to the abattoirs.

As we leave the paddock we come across a black heifer walking around in circles like a mad thing.

'Too many marshmallows,' says the dealer, pointing out a weed in the paddock that looks as much like a marshmallow as I look like a pineapple.

'Must be good stuff,' I say.

'Help yourself,' he says. 'Take as much as you like.'

I pass, thanks all the same.

AGE SHALL NOT WEARY THEM

I drop in on some friends on the mid-north coast of New South Wales. They have a house and a bit of an orchard, but most of the property is heavily treed mountain terrain, which they're very protective of. They'd rather own a forest that'll never be cleared than a clearing that'll never be forested.

Another thing they're protective of is their horse, Upkeep. He's about a hundred years old and he likes apples, peeled and quartered, if you please. He accepts the presence of *The Parrot* in his paddock as if it were the most natural of God's creatures, even coming up to give Charlie's portrait a kiss. In the middle of the night I hear him snuffling around outside so I open the door and off he gallops, snorting and tossing his head with great affection. Under a full moon on a fresh winter's night the old horse wants to play.

The next day I drive to Harrington and walk the seawall right to the end, where I've spotted a very agile rock fisherman spinning for tailor. With some difficulty I clamber out over the boulders to where he is fishing and greet him with a compliment about how fit he is.

'The Doc reckons I haven't got twelve months to live,' he responds.

He's sixty-eight years old and six months ago he was diagnosed with oesophageal cancer and given a year to live. He used to be a carpenter, but some years ago he retired to care for his wife who has emphysema. The first thing she said when he broke the news of his own illness to her was, 'How dare you get sick. You're my carer.' His voice is full of compassion sharing this confidence.

He's always been an active man and his grandkids think he's

bullet-proof. He knows he's not. He's been through various treatments, including chemotherapy, and takes off his cap to show me his thinned-out snowy hair. There is another operation he could have but the doctors have told him it would make little difference.

'If you don't have it you'll die,' his specialist said. 'And if you have it you'll die anyway.'

He hasn't told his grandkids yet.

At the moment he's off chemotherapy and feeling good. Even his taste buds are working again, and he tells me he ate a whole bar of chocolate on his last drive to Sydney, piece by delicious piece. He looks like a naughty schoolboy when he says this.

His next visit to the specialist is on my birthday and I tell him I'll spare a thought. He tells me he'll do likewise. I negotiate my way back to the easier ground and take a backward look. He gives me the thumbs up. I return it and the waves crash against the rocks.

In Taree I catch up with some family I didn't know I had. While I'd been doing some radio in Port Macquarie a woman had rung the station claiming she was my second cousin, since her father married my grandfather's sister. Her father was eighty-nine years old and it turned out he knew my namesake well. I've never known much about my Uncle Monty because he was killed in Papua New Guinea during World War II and the subject was too painful for my grandmother to talk about. So I decide to backtrack a bit and pay a visit.

The family is a real treat. The whole tribe has turned out and I'm made to feel like I've been a part of this family forever. The table's full of food and the old man's home brew is produced and songs are sung and there's plenty of laughter.

He tells me Monty wasn't killed immediately from the machine gun wounds to his belly – 'Twenty-one times, they shot him,' was as far as my grandmother could get before she'd break into tears – but died in his mate's arms after he crossed the river. I suggest he must have been leaking like a sieve, and we all laugh because it's easier than the alternative.

He's a joy, the old man, and when I tell him he'll be in the book I'm writing about the trip, which should be finished in about a year, he asks me if I couldn't hurry it up a bit, and his eyes are full of merry and I feel like I know him well.

We hug when I leave and he says to me, 'It's a long time since I've held a Dwyer in these arms.' And I believe it meant a lot to him.

And I know it meant a lot to me.

THE LOLLIPOP MAN

On a hot day in the middle of nowhere-in-particular I'm stopped at a roadworks plant by a lollipop man with his stop-and-go sign. The stretch of road under repair is long and most of the plant is well off in the distance. Only the lollipop man is in my vicinity.

He's short and chunky, with a round face under a floppy white hat, and he's leaning on his stop-and-go sign in such a way that if either lets go, both will fall. Typical of lollipop men he isn't prone to extravagant gestures, and when I pull up in front of him he just nods slightly as if to say, 'Yeah, that'll do ya,' and goes back to his leaning, which he hadn't stopped anyway.

I put *The Parrot* in park and keep the motor idling, watching him for any sign of progress up ahead. He has a two-way radio in his spare hand and every now and then I hear some communication uttered on the thing, and once or twice he even responds, though it's hard to determine what's being said.

He doesn't look like he's about to change the status quo in a hurry so I turn the motor off.

In the distance I can make out the bitumen sprayer and the

multi-wheeled rollers and other machines all doing their thing, and the air is rich with the smell of tar. Twice he waves a truck loaded with gravel through with the slightest of nods.

After a time he straightens up from his lollipop and walks over to my window.

'They're just laying a stretch now,' he says. 'Won't be too much longer.'

'That's cool; I'm in no hurry.'

At this he nods and looks behind me to where another car has just pulled up. Apparently approving of its park, he nods again and leans back on his sign, this time about three metres from my window.

I remember once, when I was a troubled teenager and showing no sign of choosing a career for myself, my father suggesting I might like to be a lollipop man.

'Reckon you could handle that job, mate?' he'd said to me. 'Looks like about the right level of stress for you.'

I look over at my lollipop man leaning on his sign. He's only a young bloke of about thirty, and it's true he doesn't look too stressed.

'What's the most interesting thing you've seen doing this job?' I ask him.

'The most interesting? Now that might be more than I can tell you,' he says in such an enigmatic way that I wonder whether he doesn't know or just doesn't care to say.

'But I can tell you sometimes I get the chicks flashing their tits as they drive through; and that's always nice.

'And one day over on the coast I was working on a bit of a back road, about thirty kilometres from the nearest town, and a bloke on a bicycle rode through wearing nothing but a helmet and his boots. Block and tackle flapping all over the place. And not a stitch on.'

I laugh, just as the two-way crackles into life.

'Yeah, that's about it,' says a voice I can hear clearly now. 'Better let Steve get his away first; he's had 'em there for a while.'

And with that my lollipop man nods his almost imperceptible nod and sends me on my way.

UNWANTED CHARITY

They tell me the Roma cattle saleyards are the largest in Australia, but it's hard to imagine how they run enough stock on the brown land thereabouts to justify that title. Apparently it's got to do with travel restrictions on road trains and B-doubles, and the town's centralised proximity to a lot of distant cattle country, but the proliferation of feedlot farming must also play a role.

I meet with a feedlot farmer with a few things to get off his chest about the way governments manage drought. He and his wife are frustrated that natural market forces aren't allowed to prevail.

'The whole issue of government funding for drought relief,' he starts, 'and cheaper freight and reduced-interest loans and this and that, isn't really helping in the longer term. If the farmer can't hold his own situation, and in a good year grow enough fodder to prepare for the next drought, then bad luck.'

He's a young man with a strong build and even stronger opinions, and when he speaks on these matters he does so with passion. After a quick tour of the property he and his wife host me for lunch – steak, of course – and both are adamant that over-subsidisation is not helping the industry. It's refreshing to hear a point of view not often attributed to farmers.

'If this happened thirty, forty years ago,' he continues, 'there'd be people going broke all over the place, which gives the smarter farmers a chance to get ahead, the younger generations a chance to come through. But there's too much propping up. Don't matter if you're as dumb as dog shit and only farming Mummy and Daddy's property because you inherited it, the government keeps giving you handouts.'

He made these comments in the interview I put to air, and caught some flak from some of his colleagues for being too harsh. Notwithstanding, there is plenty of support for his views among the farming community, and this was by no means the last time I heard this theory tabled.

'What about all the other small businesses in town?' he asks me hypothetically. 'They're suffering just as much but they don't receive support from the government. So why should the man on the land get handouts?

'Farmers are sole traders, it's private enterprise, and if the government needs to keep pouring money into farming to keep the show on the road then it's subsidising a non-feasible asset.'

Point taken, but maybe the small businesses in town have got their eyes on a different carrot. With the Surat Basin being identified as one of the world's great reserves of coal seam gas, there's a lot of interest in the area. Like many regional towns in the vicinity of a resource, Roma's fortunes are changing. Real estate sales and rentals have 'gone north', I'm told the caravan park has been bought in its entirety by one of the mining companies to accommodate staff, and you can buy a bottle of Grange Hermitage for seven hundred dollars in one of the town's eateries. The town's in a state of flux and it feels like something big is about to happen.*

* At the time of publication, news had just broken of a formidable foreign offer for one of our larger stakeholders in the Surat Basin gas fields, which, at very least, showed the rest of the world was on the case. Could this be the start of the 'something big' I sensed?

CEREAL CRISES

I meet a farmer out there who cries in his breakfast cereal. Depression occasioning suicide is the silent epidemic that affects rural communities nationwide in times of drought, and this man was certainly exhibiting some worrying symptoms.

'Once I get going I'm fine,' he tells me, 'but first thing, with the whole day ahead of me, honestly sometimes I come out here to have breakfast and I'll have tears rolling down my cheeks at thought of having to face another day.'

Later his wife tells me she'd never heard him say that before, knew he was badly depressed but never knew was crying in his cereal. (I considered telling her I'd had cereal like that too, but thought better of it.) He says he opened up to me because he'd seen me on television and decided I was pretty feminine as far as blokes go. A bit of a girl, in other words.

'Women are better listeners than men, as a rule,' he says, comfortingly. 'They listen with their eyes. Men roll their eyes, even if they're in the same position.'

The statistics confirm that men are more vulnerable to depression because they're less likely to seek help than women, and show a marked increase in the number of men over twenty-five falling victim to suicide with every year a drought is prolonged. Some figures have that number as high as one every three days somewhere in the country.

I ask him what he thinks is causing his depression and he dismisses the drought as a cause. This surprises his wife again, but I remember something from a previous career: that it's not an uncommon symptom of depression to avoid acknowledging the real problem.

'I started farming because I liked growing things,' he says. 'Then it got bigger and bigger and now I seem to spend the whole day going around making sure everyone is doing the jobs I used to like to do.

'Like the story about the man who liked to fish. And one day the bank manager talked him into buying a boat so he could catch more fish, then another boat so he could catch even more fish and make more money. Then pretty soon he had a fleet of boats and no time to fish anymore. So the bank manager said he must buy more boats so he could afford to hire someone else to run his business, so he could once again have the time to sit on the banks of the river and fish.'

For some reason that reminds me of the old adage about banks giving you an umbrella when it's sunny and taking it away when it rains.

'I just don't feel as though I've got a real purpose in my life,' the farmer continues. 'It used to be getting the kids through school, but now they're gone I've got a big void.'

'Do you ever contemplate suicide?'

'All the time,' he says. 'It'd be a lovely way to end it. But what stops me is imagining what people will think of me, of my family, because I jumped off. So I can't see myself doing it. Not today.'

When I leave, his wife tells me she knows he isn't out of the woods yet, but I like to think they'll pull through. It makes no sense otherwise. She really should change brands of cereal though.

Then I meet a wheat farmer with a Photoshopped picture hanging on his office wall, of Sydney Harbour drained and planted out to wheat.

'I just love wheat,' he tells me. 'I eat, sleep and breathe wheat. It's my passion, it's my hobby, it's my work, it's my sport, it's everything.'

I ask him what state the Australian wheat industry is in at the moment.

'The last time we saw this much excitement in wheat was back in the early seventies when the old USSR finally admitted – with communism – it couldn't feed itself, and wheat went from about fifty dollars a tonne to a hundred.

'And in real terms it didn't shift from there until the last twelve months when the world economy and the demand for ethanol means we're consuming more grain than we can produce.'

'So what's your take on ethanol? Is it a viable energy source given the amount of grain needed to produce it?'

'It's a complete farce. If we think we're going to solve our energy needs by growing more crops we've got rocks in our heads. If man wants to keep producing enough food and fibre to keep himself fed, he can't afford to open up any more land, and ethanol's only going to escalate that problem and put more pressure on fragile land. The environmental movement shouldn't have anything to do with ethanol; they should be knocking it at every turn.'

'That doesn't seem to be a concern in the US at present.'

'No it doesn't. And surprise, surprise, it's political. Americans produce three hundred million tonnes of corn, a hundred million tonne of which is now used for ethanol; it's mandated. But no politician's going to withdraw support for ethanol, because the public sees it as a green energy source.

'On the other side of the coin the mid-west is going through the biggest boom in its history at the moment, and with the rest of the country about to go into recession it's going to be two different countries over there: the mid-west, and the rest. People are coming back to small towns, there's only 2 per cent unemployment – that's where the wealth is, the confidence.

'But ethanol is not the answer. If we want to get serious about addressing our energy needs for the next hundred years we've got to start developing options such as solar, wind, hydrogen and the like, and forget about these short-term half-fixes.'

And it's hard to ignore the words of a man who's speaking out against something he profits from.

WATER WISER

Maryborough's a pretty town but it always reminds me of bossy aunts and 'God Save the Queen'. Maybe it's all the old Queenslanders – early Australian architecture typically featuring high-set timber homes with corrugated-iron roofing and large verandahs, often decorated with extravagant staircases and ornamental finishes – or maybe it's because P. L. Travis conceived *Mary Poppins* there, I don't know.

In contrast, its seaside satellite city, Hervey Bay, is a cheeky little parvenu, largely thanks to the whale-watching boom, and its proximity to Fraser Island, the world's largest sand island.

While the area hasn't got the water problems much of the country is facing – though there is plenty of debate about the controversial Traveston Dam project – the rapid growth of Hervey Bay has created a few water issues at the other end of the line.

But cometh the hour cometh the man/woman/company (take your pick), and here an autonomous wing of the local council is breaking all the rules with truly impressive results.

The first example of its ingenuity came back in the late 1980s when Hervey Bay needed to look at expanding its sewage output. After determining the ocean outlet option was too expensive, the company decided to buy a block of land and build a terrestrial reservoir to handle the effluent – a relatively new concept at the time.

Then came the first of the value-added initiatives.

'Sugar cane,' a representative from the company tells me. 'When we purchased the farm, about a thousand acres, there was an existing dry-land cane farm on it. So we called for tenders from cane growers in the district to work the land, and only one farmer put his hand up. And he went from the worst farmer in the district to winning the sugar cane productivity award a couple of times.

'So when we built the second effluent dam all the sugar cane growers put their hands up,' he adds. 'Plus the golf course and the local turf farm as well.'

These days there's a diversity of agricultural concerns using the recycled water right along the pipeline joining the two effluent dams they now operate, all thriving on the back end of Hervey Bay, as it were.

Next came the Australian hardwood plantations, which could benefit from the recycled water in times of plenty, yet which wouldn't die if there was no excess after the commercial farmers used their priority allocations. Now they've got a value-added crop that also helps keep the air clean.

Then the company developed a system to harvest the town's stormwater in order to keep their sewage fresh and avoid the build-up of unpleasant odours. During the day sewage flows more freely, allowing aerobic bacteria to do their job and keep the odours down. But overnight, while we're not using the system, the sewage tends to stop in one great plug, encouraging the anaerobic bacteria to produce the evil-smelling sulphuric gases we all prefer to avoid. So effectively they sweetened their sewage with stormwater that would otherwise have gone out to sea.

The latest project he tells me about is a partnership with another company that intends to use the effluent ponds to cultivate native fish for processing into aquaculture food.

'Water's a scarce resource in Australia,' he continues, 'and every time we use it we add another set of values.'

'Do you think water's managed well in this country?'

'No. I think the problem is an institutional one. There are a lot of competing demands, a lot of competing players, and the net result is when you have times of drought, like we've got now, we don't have one single entity prepared to stand up and take responsibility for it. We need reform, badly.'

'The state boundaries don't help, either.'

'No they don't, but I'll tell you a little story about water management,' he says, with a cheeky grin. 'Australia thinks it has issues with rivers crossing state boundaries. I can tell you the Nile crosses various national boundaries. And one year the Sudan sent word to Egypt that they were going to dam the Nile. And Egypt sent them back a telegram saying, "If you build a dam, we'll bomb it." That, to me, is the ultimate in catchment management.'

CANARIES AND CANE

She is ninety-four years old and she breeds Yorkshire canaries. One of her birds has just won Best Bird in Show and I offer congratulations and suggest she must have a feel for Yorkies.

She smiles and enjoys the flattery for an instant, then changes her tune and frowns.

'I didn't think he'd win,' she says. 'All he does at home is fidget and fuss. I can't get him to do anything. Here he was well behaved.'

Her voice is thin and gravelly like a country road, and rises and falls about the same. She's sitting on a chair facing her well-behaved boy, and her eyes are sparkling mischievous. She watches me sit next to her and says nothing.

'He's in good song right now,' I say.

'Yes, yes,' she says. 'He seems pleased with himself.'

It's a cold, wet day in Mackay, and later that afternoon I walk into a lounge bar to find a flight crew from one of our national carriers shivering and wrapped in blankets and even newspapers, I swear. The next day the papers confirm it never climbed beyond 11.8 degrees, making it the coldest maximum on record, and breaking the previous record set in 1958 by over 2 degrees.

My canary lady would have still been a young woman when that record was set, probably raising the last of her family. It's unlikely she'd have seen herself almost fifty years later sitting alone at the show, proud of a bird she'd raised. She probably took over the canaries when her husband died, because it seemed like the right thing to do to keep his birds alive. Now they're as much a part of her life as he was.

Outside, the hardy show-goers are in good spirits regardless, almost as if they're determined to enjoy themselves even more to spite the weather. Or perhaps the enjoyment isn't forced at all, but a genuine response to variation, a departure from life's uniformed march.

I'm gathering vox pops and I put the microphone to the man who runs the plastic duck stall and suggest he should liberate the ducks in the muddy walkway. He picks up the ball without missing a beat.

'I tried that but they kept escaping to go on the rides,' he says, deadpan.

I suspect he's half-pissed and ask him how long he's been doing the ducks.

'Too long,' he tells me. 'Ten years? We go up and down the east coast, from Cairns to Ballarat, Ballarat back to Cairns, then back again.' I get the picture: he's ready for a change. I move on.

I find a girl of about four years eating fairy floss. I ask her what rides she's been on, and in an irresistibly earnest voice she tells me she hasn't been on any rides because her Dad wouldn't let her.

'Or my Mum,' she remembers, frowning.

A grown man with a big soft toy under his arm tells me it's definitely a bull, not a moose, but he can't remember which game he played to win it. His mate comes to the rescue.

'You know, the one where you make the fish swim faster over the top of the thing and then the arm comes down and if you're quick enough you win,' he says. The winner confirms this with a satisfied nod. Now we all know.

A mother watches her children squealing and whizzing around on some sort of open-carriage ride. She's smiling broadly and the raindrops are wetting her upturned face.

'They must be getting drenched,' I say, stating the obvious.

'Yeah,' she says, not taking her eyes off them. 'This is their third go.'

'Not tempted to go up with the kids?'

'Not in this weather. They're crazy.' And she laughs through the rain.

Back inside the bird exhibit shed my canary breeder is worried about the rain. I ask her if there's been too much and concern clouds her face like a storm.

'It's terrible,' she says. 'They won't be able to get the cane in for crushing. And they've already had to put it off twice.'

She is ninety-four years old and she's seen this happen before. Rain at this time of year makes the fields too boggy to harvest. Mackay's crop isn't the largest in Australia, but including Sarina and Proserpine the area produces about a quarter of the nation's sugar cane crush. Operating at capacity the plants need about twenty-three weeks to process the crop, regardless of when the harvest begins. This means every week lost at the start of the harvest waiting for the fields to dry must be added on to the end, and the farmers run the risk of clashing with the wet season. If the monsoonal rains come before the cane is in, there's nothing to be done but leave it there.

She also knows that cane is a ratoon crop, meaning it will regrow after harvest just like a lawn will regrow after being mowed. This allows farmers to get numerous crops from the one planting. But it also means if it's left standing in the field it can stimulate its own regrowth and take off again, using its own reserves of sucrose to fuel the new growth spurt. This often lowers sucrose levels, which is not good, since farmers get better prices for higher sugar levels.

She may also know that the by-product from the cane crush is called bagasse, and is being used for power generation and ethanol distillation. It's hard to imagine these developments would excite someone who has been around longer than household electricity and almost as long as the Model-T Ford, but she would certainly support anything to help the growers.

She asks me why I'm so interested in an old woman, and I tell her I'm doing some radio.

'Have you heard of Charles Wooley?'

'No,' she says.

'He's a very attractive man,' I tell her. 'Do you want me to send him up to you?'

That's when she tells me how old she is.

'You could probably still handle him, couldn't you?'

'I expect so,' she says, and laughs the most delicious little laugh I've heard in years, a sound that carries every flavour of woman that man ever got lucky enough to taste.

She is ninety-four years old and she breeds canaries, she cares about the cane farmers, and her heart is still as young as the breeze.

A SLIPPERY WEEKEND

This one goes down the sink like a raw egg.

I leave a cold and wet Mackay hoping I'm not seeing a snapshot of tropical north Queensland when climate change starts getting nasty.

Next stop is Airlie Beach, another place that doesn't work in the wet. Everything about Airlie – the colour of the water, the bustle of tourists on the street, the balmy palm tree nights – depends on the sun doing a full day's work. With the sun off sick the place feels sad. The outdoor cafes are empty, people walk by wearing ski jackets, there is no buzz.

I move on, calling into a couple of the smaller beaches as I head north, and a recurrent theme starts to emerge from talks with the locals. They can no longer afford to buy waterfront real estate in their own towns. We're used to this in the cities, of course, but it seems ludicrous up here so far from the capitals.

'It's the fly-in, fly-out mentality,' the mayor of Bowen tells me. 'You're in the middle of the coal basin here, and most of the miners work a four-on, four-off roster, so a lot of them live on the coast and fly to work.

'That, and all the southern investment money pretty much means locals can't afford to own houses in their own towns.'

'So where do they go?'

'Some go inland for the tree change. Many of the people in these old fishing villages are pensioners, and I guess a lot of them move into retirement homes until they're ready for the sky change. And the rest are forced to rent. Or form family partnerships in order to buy, which is happening more and more up this way.'

Bowen's hosting the production of an epic Australian movie. There's a couple of big names in the thing who must be accounting for most of the budget, because the mayor tells me they're pretty tight with their purse strings, playing the 'Bowen's getting a lot of publicity out of this' card at every negotiation.

I wander down to the set to look for some off-Broadway action. I find flag-waving Fred, a man on a mission. For sixteen months he's been travelling the country with the new flag he's designed for us, honing his spiel. I'll spare you a sample, out of common courtesy; suffice to say Fred is dedicated and proud of his flag. Google 'flagoz' if you're interested.

I also talk to a security man guarding a toilet block who has seen cattle taught to walk backwards off the wharf, and bomb craters created with excavators and black spray paint, but no sign of the female lead. The male lead's been a big hit with the locals, getting out and about and mixing with them without fuss, but his love interest has been conspicuously shy. The guard tells me he dreams about her. I tell him that's what he's expected to do.

One person who has seen the elusive female star at close quarters is an eight-year-old girl I meet. Her mother tells me when the girl came home from her big day as an extra on set, rubbing shoulders with Hollywood royalty, she asked her what the highlight was. The girl told her the dingo pups.

The mayor has had 'Bowenwood' painted on the town's water reservoir in big letters in the same font as the LA version. He's copping some grief from the locals, who probably see it as too pretentious, but he says he hopes it will attract more movie productions to the area. Then he grins broadly.

I leave the star-studded Bowenwood and head further north. In Townsville I hook up with an old mate and we go for a drink at an upmarket bar on the waterfront. At one stage I find myself suddenly surrounded by young women. At last, I think, my due. But then I'm introduced to the main attraction, standing next to me. He's a footballer, considered by many to be the best going around at the moment. He's also not the least bit interested in me: I was the wrong sex.

I catch a cab back to the van and meet a black South African woman with a string of degrees and four kids, who can't get a better job than driving a taxi. It just hasn't worked for her here. Australia has failed her. The cab fare is fourteen-something dollars and I tell her to keep the change out of twenty, which I would always do unless the driver gives me the shits. She refuses to accept it, believing I'm offering it as charity. Australia has failed her again.

I go to bed feeling weird, and wake well before dawn with somebody shining a torch in the front window of the Hymer. I sit up and he lopes off, unconcernedly, wearing a towel wrapped around his head as if he were a woman fresh from washing her hair. For a moment I consider stepping out and challenging him, then change my mind. What worthwhile thing could that achieve?

Sleep eludes me for the rest of the night as I ponder the whole universal energy concept. Does weird attract weird? Is the itinerant nature of this trip taking its toll? I don't know, but I know I need to snap out of this.

WHEN YOU HAVEN'T GOT A GUN

I have a confession to make: I used to be a spearfisherman. Way back in my callow youth I was, for a brief period, a professional fisherman. And occasionally, when the weather was too good to be setting nets, I'd venture out to the reef to shoot Coral Trout and others for fun and profit.

Coral Trout are beautiful fish to spear because they're curious by nature and have an obliging tendency to swim up from the depths to meet you. The hardest part of the job was keeping the sharks off the fish you'd already shot. Occasionally they got so cheeky we had to straight-shaft the buggers, which is to shoot them with the barbs removed from the spear so it goes in, but pulls out freely. Unkind, yes – barbs or not – and I know it would be Karma if I was taken by a shark as penance, but it was either that or blow them away with a power head (a spear loaded with a live cartridge), so we fancied we were doing them a favour.

I offer this little insight into my background because it's school holidays and my ten-year-old daughter, Benino, has just flown up to join me in Cairns. Naturally she wants to visit the reef, so I book us in for one of the many daytrips on offer. The last time I tried this, the boat sank before we even left the harbour and I had my first and only experience salvage-diving. But these days the industry's a little more organised, and the trip involves catching an enormous catamaran out to a permanently-anchored pontoon for a day of snorkelling, scuba diving, helicopter riding, and as many other reef activities as you can cram into five hours.

Now, I do understand this is the only way to give large numbers of people a taste of one of the great wonders without loving it to death. But I'm not good at the whole tour group thing, especially revisiting something I know so well.

But my daughter's taking it all in with wide eyes – not what her father's trying to teach her, mind; it's the twenty-year-old backpackers' orientation speech she's lapping up – and by the time we reach the pontoon she's itching with excitement.

I'm itching as well, but I'm not quite sure why. It's been over twenty-five years since I dived on the reef and I'm really not sure what to expect, or how much it's changed.

As soon as I hit the dive platform I realise what it is that's itching. It's my trigger finger. They've been feeding a couple of Maori Wrasse so they come up onto the platform and swim through the legs of the delighted tourists. As party tricks go it's a big hit and everybody loves it. I'm almost drooling. In their natural state, wrasse are tricky propositions because they hole up in caves as soon as they sense danger, and you have to be lucky to get them out. And here was a twenty-five-kilo beauty I could have picked off between my daughter's calves.

I manage to control this inappropriate urge and slip over the side to have a look around, and for whatever my highly unscientific appraisal is worth, it doesn't appear to have changed much since the last time I was here; a little light on colour, perhaps, but that's impossibly subjective since I've never dived this patch of reef before. We've all heard about coral bleaching and Crown of Thorns starfish, and there's been growing concern over fertilisers and other agricultural pollutants filtering out from the coast and causing harm, but here I could see no obvious signs of degradation, either from the aforementioned dangers or the increased traffic.

Only problem was the old 'urge' kept recurring, and each time I saw a trout I found myself tensing up and preparing to go into dive mode. I needed to get out of the water before somebody saw me and locked me in the hold.

Unfortunately Benino was having such a good time in the water she didn't want to get out, and insisted I join her on the afternoon dive along the drop-off where the reef meets the blue water.

So there I was, gliding along in mid-water like it was a quarter of a century ago, getting well carried away with myself, rolling down to meet trout halfway up, sliding through crevasses looking for crayfish feelers, and generally behaving like a moron until my daughter tugged my flippers and told me to get back to the group: our teenage dive guide straight off the plane from Scotland was going crook. She's got me tagged as a danger to myself if not others and my own daughter's on her side.

Oh my, sometimes I understand why old people get pissed off when we assume they don't know what they're doing.

BENINO

Benino likes to identify road kill as we drive along. That's not her real name, by the way. I choose to live in the public eye; she can make her own choices. But she was always interested in death. One time when she was about four years old I took her fishing. We caught a small tailor and she watched with fascination as I cut it up for bait. Then we caught another and I asked her if we should throw that one back, since we had enough fresh bait.

'No, cut him,' she said, and handed me the knife.

A potential suitor would be well advised to take note of that personality trait.

Now she sits beside me in the car, pointing out the animals that never made it.

'Another dingo,' she says.

'You, sure?' I ask. 'Looked like a sleeping wallaby to me.'

'Nope. Dead dingo. Holding its breath.'

She's referring to the animal being bloated up in the sun, and I'm pleased to note she has a sense of the absurd.

We're driving up to The Daintree, another trip I haven't taken for over a quarter of a century, back when I was a professional net fisherman – the spear fishing was only an occasional diversion – so I knew the area pretty well. When we reach the river my daughter says she'd like to do a boat cruise.

'Why don't we hire a dinghy and I'll show you around?'

'No,' she says. 'I'd rather go with a real boat driver.'

Here we go again. Children have no concept of their parents as anything but parents.

'What are you afraid of?' I ask. 'Crocodiles?'

'No,' she says. 'Well, maybe. I'd just rather be in a bigger boat.'

I remember frightening her mother when I took her to the Northern Territory for our honeymoon, thinking she'd appreciate the experience. At that time I could access places most non-Aboriginal people could never see, right along northern Arnhem Land through some of Australia's most unforgettable country, thanks to my job on TV.

Unfortunately, she didn't warm to the crocodiles at all, and wasn't too keen on the snakes, stingers, midges and bush tucker either. I don't think I'd be exaggerating to say she never let go enough to really enjoy it, and when we got back among our smart city friends she made good mileage out of the fact that her husband had taken her camping with the blackfellas for her honeymoon.

Now I'm seeing little signs of her mother's resistance to letting go developing in my daughter, and it saddens me. She used to be a courageous little girl. Now she's growing cautious, afraid to try new things, worried about what will happen. I wonder if this is just a natural phase, or a result of less influence from me than she had as a younger child. I settle on the former since the latter is too painful to own.

We cross the ferry to Cape Tribulation and play tourists for a bit. A rainforest walk costs me nearly fifty dollars for the two of us. I'm told the price is high because of the insurance premiums the operators have to pay for public liability. It's a point raised several times on the trip.

We camp at one of the beachside caravan parks not yet overrun by development and go for a walk along the beach. This is a rarity for my daughter because she doesn't do walking. She believes it's boring and uncool. Today she's making an exception.

'Look!' she says. 'Soldier crabs.'

'No they're not.'

'Oh, yes they are.'

'Oh, no they're not.'

So we scramble around like, well, two kids, and catch one for identification. It's a little sand crab of some description. I push her for an admission of defeat.

'Go on, say it: I was right and you were wrong.'

'I can't. It won't come out.'

'Yes you can. Come on.'

'Okay. You were right and I was wrong,' she says at the speed of light so it's unintelligible. I make to throttle her and she runs off squealing and laughing.

It's just a silly little moment between a man and his daughter, on a holiday in Far North Queensland. I wonder if it's one she'll remember.

I know she'll remember diving on the reef, and seeing a cassowary cross the road with two little chicks at Mission Beach. She'll probably remember taking the Skyrail trip from Cairns to Kuranda. Maybe she'll remember catching a barra, and seeing a crocodile or two. In other words the primary features.

But will she remember the gentler moments, the fainter colours that give background to the features?

Knowing Benino, she'll probably only remember the best ice-cream.

NO ROOM FOR GHOSTS

It's four in the morning and I'm outside the lovely old pub at Yungaburra freezing my tits off while I wait for *The Parrot* to warm up. I'm supposed to be in my room inside, waiting for Maud the ghost to visit me, but I think it's too cold for a ghost to be out tonight. It's certainly too cold inside the pub. I woke about half an hour ago and went for a bit of a wander, but all I could think of was getting into the Hymer and cranking up the gas heating system. So if Maud is planning a visit she'll have to come out here to me where it's warm. Or will be soon.

How are you supposed to attract a ghost anyway? They gave me the old honeymoon suite because that's where she'd been sighted a few times. Heaven forbid: me in a honeymoon suite. That's enough to frighten any ghost. I did hear a few floorboards creak, the odd window rattle, but saw nothing you'd call other-worldly; like a bride, for instance.

Maud Williams Kehoe was the licensee of the pub from the early 1900s till she died in 1971. She started running the original inn back in 1907 when she was only sixteen years old, and carried on as the driving force of the place once the existing two-storey building was constructed in about 1912. She married the stationmaster, Jack Kehoe, in 1914, when they must have been two of the most happening people in the district: Jack in charge of the brand new railway station, and Maud running the pub.

There's a frost on the ground outside, by the way. Far North Queensland and there's ice underfoot. Somebody slap me with a fish and tell me I'm mistaken.

To get to *The Parrot* at this hour of the morning without waking any of the others I had to climb down the fire escape, which is an iron ladder propped against the rear sundeck. There's one just like it at the front as well, only that one lands in the middle of the footpath on the main street! Both would claim lives if they had to be used in an emergency. You'd be better off taking your chances with the fire. But it's got some charm: great cavernous rooms, beautiful silky oak joinery including a grand old staircase, fireplaces, front bar full of character, and ghosts to boot! Allegedly.

I'm not even sure I believe in ghosts, although I did go out with a woman one time who told a spine-tingling ghost story that was very hard to disbelieve. It was set in an old hotel as well and, according to her, a young boy turned on her bedroom light in the middle of the night and they had a conversation. Then in the morning when she mentioned it over breakfast her host said, 'Oh yes, that would have been So-and-so,' the little boy who'd died there of something or other, death most likely, and then the host went on to describe the details of the visitation without being told. Spooky.

There's supposed to be the ghost of a young boy here as well, who hangs around outside in the backyard where I'm parked, according to the yard manager, at least. He reckons he saw him one night while he was putting out the garbage, but yardies are notorious for being pissed most of their working lives and no doubt see all sorts of weirdness out by the garbage bins.

Anyway, I doubt you'd see any apparition outside this morning through the condensation of your breath. Fancy that: I'm on a ghost hunt in the tropics and I'll have to call it off because it's too cold. Guess I'll just have to remain a sceptic for a bit longer.

LOST

I've just spent the last week in and around the Atherton Tableland while the show was broadcast from Mareeba, and now the crew has left I feel quite strange. Maybe it was too much time chasing ghosts, or too many late nights with Charlie and our producer, but whatever it was I'm having trouble feeling the ground beneath my feet right now.

I lived in Mareeba for a short spell. I was a nurse at the hospital. Can't say I was ever much good at it, though – too many sputum mugs and bedpans for my liking. And corpses. I remember performing the last rites on more than my share of uncooperative stiffs, and for some reason I can't recall I also participated in quite a number of post-mortems. It's the business side of death, and not nearly as creepy as you might imagine. When the life leaves a body it becomes lifeless, whatever your spiritual inclinations.

The tobacco industry was still going well then, and I lived with some other nurses in a big house on a tobacco farm. Tobacco's finished in Mareeba now. Some say it was bad management. Others say the multinationals squeezed the local growers out. All I know is the smell of tobacco leaves drying in a barn is far sweeter than the smell of a man dying of emphysema.

Today the legitimate drug grown here is coffee. We visit a very modern set-up outside Mareeba run by an ex-army officer from Zimbabwe. He tells me Mugabe tapped him on the shoulder when it was time to go, and said, 'There's no future for you in this country, sonny.' He took his advice and left immediately.

When we meet he shakes my hand and looks into my eyes as if they are not so much a window to my soul as a door he kicks in without ceremony.

He claims to be the only coffee producer in the country to be making a profit. His secret? Outrageous pricing. I suggest the struggle to position his product so highly in a competitive marketplace would be nothing to a man of his background. He shrugs and smiles faintly. I'm expecting a tap on the shoulder at any stage.

I meet a publican with a mess of children who was told by his father, who was told by his father, 'Never sell the pub because it will give you somewhere to teach your kids the ropes, right from wrong.'

Now each of the kids has done time in the front bar and the restaurant, in the mix of good and bad you can only find in a public house. And he's rightfully proud of them, but worries about whether they'll want to stay in the trade.

'You'd think I'd jag one publican out of six kids, wouldn't you?' he asks me.

I hope he's right. It'd kill him to sell the pub after three generations.

My producer looks up some family he's never met and learned

more about his father than he ever wanted to know. He needs some company, so we go for a drink at an old pub that had copped a fair hiding from Cyclone Larry. And it seems entirely appropriate to be having a beer with a man whose foundations have just been shaken, in a pub with a broken façade.

The last thing I do on the tablelands is drive *The Parrot* in the rodeo parade and throw lollies to the kids, which should be enough happiness to lighten even the heaviest heart.

Then I leave town with the intention of getting a good chunk of the next day's drive done before I camp. I don't get ten kilometres down the road before a great weariness ambushes me. I sleep badly and wake feeling like an eel: slippery and hard to pin down.

And somewhere in the midst of all that lot it feels as though a spring unwound.

DOUBLEDOGS IN THE BADLANDS

There's nothing quite like a near-death experience to re-focus the mind.

Leaving the Atherton Tableland I followed the Kennedy Highway south along a single, raggedy strip of bitumen cutting the red land in two. On either side of the road was a dirt verge about a metre or so wide, which dropped down to a rough clearing back to the scrub line. The sun was warm and I was enjoying the drive.

Then around the corner ahead of me came a road train. He was belting along at a frightening clip and using the whole road, so I eased *The Parrot* over to the verge so I was half on, half off the road, expecting the truck to do the same, since there wasn't a lot of space for either of us to use. It was very nearly a fatal assumption.

They say in armed combat you know the difference between random enemy fire and being specifically targeted. I fancy it was the same sensation. This guy was playing chicken with me and had no intention of moving over. Only problem was I didn't twig until we were almost kissing. Then I had no option but to throw the Hymer into the never-never and hope there was nothing nasty out there. He passed by in a thunderous whoosh, seemingly unperturbed, with not even a blast of his horn to acknowledge he'd seen me. So much for thinking he was targeting me.

The same scenario was played out several times more that morning, though I was prepared after the first skirmish and also better sighted, so I had time to find somewhere safe to ease off the road. But it seems the rules have changed out there.

I pull in at the next road stop and raise the subject. The response is strong and vocal.

'Yeah, there are some idiots, out there,' one customer says. 'Cowboys with guns fifty metres long.'

Another man tells me he knows of drivers who won't work with that particular transport company because of the cavalier culture among the drivers.

'Like everybody, they have to compete with the mines for staff,' he says, 'which is a cute twist, since they're carting for the mines. So they're getting kids barely off their P-plates and training them up. These kids throw their girlfriends in the cab, crank the music up, and away they go.

'Sooner or later someone'll get killed. And then they might do something about the road.'

I drop in to the local cop shop and ask the duty officer if he thinks it's a cultural problem with that company.

'No, I don't think so,' he says. 'You'll always get one or two rogues spoiling it for the rest. But the thing about the roads out here is you have to drive to the conditions. And when you see a road train approaching you pull over.'

'What if there's no room? Or it's wet and you need to keep one wheel on?'

'That's when we get problems,' he says, citing the old chestnut, education, as one of the keys.

And the same default position is supported by Main Roads, who advise on their website (and on roadside signs, I saw later) to give way to the trucks by pulling right off the road. Which makes perfect sense, of course, but it also means that for all intents and purposes our single-lane outback roads now have a government-sanctioned commercial priority.

I ask the police officer if there's anything they can do to control it.

'Not really. Even if we can catch them at it, and make the charge stick – it's such a minor infringement: failure to share the road I think it is – it's hardly worth the effort. Better to keep out of their road.'

Which is exactly what I'll be doing from here on in, but something is definitely amiss out there. The mining companies aren't being held to account, the state government seems reluctant to redistribute royalties to marginal population areas, and the roads are going to hell.

A little further on I stop to talk to a gang of seismic surveyors. They're rolling out cable beside the road, kilometre after kilometre, along which sensor rods are pushed into the ground and attached to the cable to take readings of the earth below.

'It's a government job,' the gang boss tells me. 'There's about thirty of us all up, in this gang. About fifty in the other. We'll be out for another few months, maybe six in all.'

'What are you looking for?'

'Anything, really. Uranium. Oil. Gas. Hot rocks.*

So there's obviously plenty of money for research. And we're not shy about ripping it out of the ground. Is it too much to expect some long-term benefits for the country we're plundering the resources from?

* Colloquial term for super-heated underground rock masses, otherwise known as geothermals, found mainly in Queensland and South Australia – and especially in the Cooper Basin – with the potential to provide Australia with a significant clean and renewable, steam-powered energy source.

GULF GRUNTER

Sometimes people blow you right off the duck's back. Just when you think you've got them pegged for one thing they turn around and do something else.

Like when they drop dead on you, for instance. Now I realise people don't usually ask to drop dead all of a sudden, but it still comes as a bit of a shock to the rest of us when they do. I guess most times it would come as something of a shock to the main player as well, except people don't usually survive death well enough to verify that for us. So it's actually the living that death affects the most, the way I see it.

My father just rang and informed me of a couple of deaths in his circle. My father's not a man given to histrionics when it comes to serious matters, only the trivial ones. So he delivers the news like this:

'Anyway, so what are you doing up there? Where are you at present?' he asks. Then before I can answer he says, 'We buried [one of his friends] yesterday. Best thing for him. He would've gone sooner if he had his way.'

Then he goes on to tell me about a bird he's trying to identify in his backyard, before he drops the second bombshell.

'And by the way, [a close relative] dropped dead up your way the other day, too.'

'I'm hoping the third one will be the mother-in-law's dog,' he continues, 'which is giving me the shits yapping its head off out there in the yard.'

Then he goes back to identifying birds.

That's how he does it. It doesn't mean he's heartless, more that he doesn't care to indulge in the sentimentality on offer. I think the old man has made friends with his own maker, so he's not too worried about anyone else's. He's had a full life and he'll go when he's told without much resistance.

A fish well played should have no fight left at the end.

Yet a well-played grunter pulled out of the southern Gulf of Carpentaria will still grunt like a pig when you land it. I wonder why it does that.

Every year the Grey Nomad migration sees the little Gulf town of Karumba stretched creaseless with sunbirds and fisherfolk. They come for the weather, which is mostly warm, and the fishing, which is mostly hot. In abundance are barramundi, Threadfin Salmon, Blue Salmon and grunter. And when they're on they get plenty.

It's a unique stretch of water, the Gulf of Carpentaria, on account of it only getting one set of tides a day. It does manage to process two sets once or twice a month, but because the mouth of the Gulf is narrower than the base, the outgoing tide runs into the next incoming tide and the water tends to go nowhere. The only other place on the planet this happens so spectacularly is the Gulf of Mexico.

Many of the migrants stay for the duration of the winter, and leave with freezers packed with fillet. Most of them aren't breaking the law; they just like to take some fish back home with them. Indeed, some of them see it as their due for making the long drive to get there in the first place, and for spending money in the town while they're there.

Without tourism there wouldn't be much to Karumba: a small commercial fishing fleet, a lead and zinc processing plant, a few brolgas, not much more.

So they come in their numbers and fill up the three caravan parks, and on any given sunny afternoon you can easily count a hundred boat trailers parked at the boat ramp car parks. It's a sight you'd more expect to see at a major holiday destination within striking range of a capital city, than out in the mangroves with the mud crabs and crocodiles.

A recent impact survey on fishing in the Gulf took everyone by surprise. In essence the survey estimated that amateur fishing alone harvested over a hundred tonnes of grunter from southern Gulf waters in 2006, compared with about a quarter of that amount by commercial fishing. In fairness grunter is not a species normally targeted by the professionals, and 2006 was a bumper year for grunter, but a hundred tonnes still seems a lot of stock to pull out of one stretch of water with fishing rods.

Along with more money for research and the development of a grunter restocking program, the survey recommended an increase in minimum size limits and a reduction in bag limits. At the time of writing, it stands at forty centimetres and ten fish per person at any one time, though when the next Gulf Management Review is released in 2008–09 don't be surprised to find a recommendation of fifty centimetres and five fish per person.

Talking to the anglers at the cleaning tables of one of the caravan parks makes it clear there is resistance to changes in the status quo.

'How do we know the figures are accurate anyway?' one woman challenges. 'They're only assumptions, based on estimates.'

'And what about the professional fishermen?' the man standing next to her asks. 'Maybe the government should be looking at buying out some fishing licences instead.'

The survey was done by a reputable environmental impact survey company, and at the time of writing the number of professional fishing licences in the Gulf was eighty-four.

I ask a man who looks and sounds a lot like Zorba the Greek if it was about the experience or the amount of fillet you can take home.

'Look, I have no problem with increasing the size limit,' he says, continuing to fillet his fish as he speaks. 'But I wouldn't come all this way for ten fillets.'

'But you could eat two hundred while you were here.'

'Yeah, but I spend a lot of money while I'm here, too.'

'What about our kids?'

'Yeah, well, that's why I say I don't mind if they put the limit up.'

And by now he's stopped filleting and he's gesturing with his knife pointing towards me to make his point, so I tell him I agree with everything he says and we all laugh. But there's obviously some strong feelings about this.

I talk with a woman who's involved in fish-rebreeding programs in the Gulf.

'You can't blame them,' she says. 'Javelin Fish, or grunter if you prefer, are a lovely table fish. And for a lot of them it's a lifestyle thing, they come and stay for the whole of winter and catch fish, especially since the road was tarred. But if we can't find a balance between the amateur catch and restocking, it has the potential to be a serious problem.'

'What would happen to Karumba if there were no grunter?'

'Biologically it would be a disaster, to take one species out of the chain, especially in such a unique environment like the Gulf. And probably it would be just as devastating for the tourism.'

But not all the fishermen are against the recommended changes.

'I feel that in the past five or six years,' one regular visitor tells me, 'the overfishing has got out of hand. And there are too many people coming up here with big freezers, expecting to take them home full, and if the weather's bad or the fish aren't biting they get very annoyed very quickly.

'We all come here for the weather and the quality of fish,' he sums up. 'We can't control the weather. But we can control the quality of fish we're going to catch in the future.'

BON APPETITE

LONDON – A rare species of long-beaked echidna native to Papua New Guinea and long thought to be extinct has been found alive by scientists.

Only one specimen of the rare egg-laying mammal, known as Attenborough's long-beaked echidna, has ever been seen by scientists, back in 1961.

But a recent expedition by British zoologists to PNG uncovered evidence that the echidna, named after renowned naturalist Sir David Attenborough, is still alive.

Seven people living in the Cyclops Mountains told the scientific team from the Zoological Society of London that they had seen the spiny creature, which is related to the platypus.

One villager had even eaten one and described it as 'delicious', The Times *newspaper reported.*

The North West Star, Thursday 19 July 2007

This little article jumps out at me while I'm reading the local paper in Mount Isa. I love the contrasting cultural approaches to the animal, and decide to hit the streets of 'The Isa' with the microphone to find out how adventurous we are with our eating habits.

Overall it seems we're a pretty boring lot. When asked to name the most unusual thing they've eaten most people nominate lambs' brains, or frogs' legs. One even says lentils, and more than one say they didn't eat anything unusual, ever. For a while the most interesting snack nominated is calf's nuts, or prairie oysters.

It isn't till I came across a couple from Argadargada, in the Northern Territory, that I hit the jackpot. They've tried everything that walks, hops, runs, flies, crawls or swims in this vast land.

And curiously, while I'm talking to them it never occurs to me that they are of Aboriginal descent, until I say I think blackfellas are shocking cooks on the strength of a Magpie Goose meal I had with a Top End mob. Then I'm not sure whether I should be embarrassed I've insulted their cooking skills and failed to recognise their obvious origins, or proud of myself that I simply don't notice skin colour when I talk to people.

Either way, it's clear our indigenous population are way ahead in the adventurous-eating stakes. Here are a few insights into our bush tucker:

- Flying Fox (Fruit Bat) tastes a bit like chicken, flavoured with whatever they've been eating; for example, if they've been on the mangoes they'll have a faint mango taste, as if slow-cooked in a mango sauce.
- Dugong is like seafood pork, and cut into steaks even looks like pork, albeit cut from a very big, round pig.
- Eating turtle will cause a tell-tale odour to be omitted through your sweat glands. Ditto goanna and Flying Fox, among others.
- Magpie Goose cooked the traditional way takes about five minutes on an open fire – just long enough to burn the feathers

off – and tastes like charred, raw meat, which is all it is (see above).

- Crocodile doesn't have a lot of taste when small, but develops a more interesting flavour somewhere between chicken and fish as it grows larger – of course, then it can be a bastard to catch.
- Snake is a lot of work for a tough result, and can have the distinctive smell of human female genitalia.
- Witchetty Grub is a slimy, greasy mouthful that will make you gag – definitely best eaten cooked, if at all.
- Plains Turkey or Bustard really does taste just like Christmas turkey and it's no wonder their numbers have dwindled.
- Black Swans are best cooked with a rock, then eaten after you've eaten the rock.
- Wombat has white flesh like pork, though with a stronger, gamier flavour.
- Echidna is a trick to prepare, and should be bled by pulling out the tongue, then the bristles should be burned off in an open fire while dousing with water to soften the flesh, finally scraping the last of the bristles away with a knife. No mention was made of gutting the thing so I can't help you there – maybe try one each way – but my source swears they're best cooked like corned beef, and taste like a cross between that and pork.

It should be noted, in case you've started salivating at the prospect of a Corned Echidna or Rock Wallaby Ragout, that you really do need to have some indigenous connection with the land to explore the menu fully.

Each state and territory has its own laws and regulating bodies responsible for the protection of our native wildlife, with the overall care and control coming under the Department for the Environment, Water, Heritage and the Arts at a federal level.

Australia has a shocking record when it comes to looking after our native flora and fauna, having consigned more plants, birds and animals to the ranks of endangered or extinct in the last two hundred years than any other country on the planet.

About the worst thing I've ever eaten was a Witchetty Grub, which made me gag violently (see above) and no doubt made for some entertaining television since it happened live to air. They may be considered a delicacy by Aborigines and Murray Cod but I'd rather eat road kill.

And just on that subject: according to my research it's not actually illegal to eat endangered species, only to harm or kill them, so presumably road kill is fair game (or foul).

Bon appetite.

RIDICULOUS TO THE SUBLIME

Boulia Camel Races 2007 – If the camel is a horse designed by a committee, then camel racing was the last item on the agenda, not addressed till after the long lunch had taken its toll on even the most sensible of board members. It's hysterical, and if you've never seen one, put it on your 'must see' list.

To begin with, the camel is a pack animal, so all it ever wants to do is get back to the rest of the gang. Accordingly they structure races around that knowledge and set the holding yards up beyond the finish line. So when the camels are released from the starting barrier they bound back to their mates, crossing the finish line en route. In theory, at least.

In practice what happens is more like this.

Let's say six camels are lined up at the starting barrier ready to go. Camel One will sit down. Camel Four will decide it's above waiting and turn around and go for a walk in the wrong direction. Camel One will be coaxed into standing back up and Camel Three will sit down. Then they'll get Camel Four back and Camel Two will bolt towards the finish line. Camel Five, sensing that's what he wanted to do all along, will bolt with Camel Two. In exasperation the starter will liberate the rest and off they'll go, loose lips flapping, great legs striding, jockeys hanging on grimly.

If a dog crosses their path they'll take off after the thing: they hate dogs. If there's a bend in the course they'll likely ignore the track and go bush. (One jockey tells me a camel he was riding a couple of years ago here went all the way into the township of Boulia, mid-race.) At any stage they're likely to veer across the track in front of the other camels, or turn around and head in the opposite direction, or sit down. It is, quite simply, racing anarchy.

The jockeys sit on small cushions precariously strapped on the downward slope of the camels back, and pray. They have reins, but they might as well be attached to the clouds, the amount of control they offer.

At the races I meet a man walking from the Spencer Gulf in South Australia to the Gulf of Carpentaria. He started walking for no reason beyond the pleasure of the challenge, but soon found himself walking to raise awareness for a charity. He was in his sixties, had been married twice and raised two families, owned successful businesses, and now he carried everything he owned in the world on his back.

'Except maybe a spare shirt back at the caravan I was living in before,' he tells me.

I ask him how he reached this liberated state of being.

'The expression I use is that I live low on the hog. I don't smoke or drink, though I've done both to excess in the past. I don't have a house so I don't need to pay a mortgage or buy furniture and what-have-you, and I don't have a car so I don't buy petrol or insurance. And what it amounts to is, because I've got no outgoings, I don't need money.'

'Was there a turning point?'

'There was no revelation, no major life-changing event. It just happened bit by bit. I had a car parked in the drive for a while and decided one day I wouldn't drive it unless I needed to. I didn't drive it for ten years, so I sold it. The other things went along the way, for the same reason: no need of them.

'One bloke stopped me early on and asked me if I was doing a spiritual pilgrimage – he was off to India to find his guru and detox – but I said, "No, I'm just going for a walk."'

'So what's out there? What are you seeing?'

'Physically, you mean?'

'Not necessarily.'

'There's nothing out there. Sometimes I just like to walk for half a day and take a photo of the horizon ahead of me, flat like a bay or an ocean, then turn around and take a photo of what's behind me, and they look exactly the same. Yet it takes me half a day to get there. And that's exciting.'

'So what's it all about, then?'

'It really isn't about anything. It's like this walk. There was no lightning flash, no awakening, it just sounded like an interesting thing to do, so I did it. So the purpose of life, if that's your question, is just to do it and enjoy it the best you can.'

BUSH POET

I reach the Blackall caravan park in the late afternoon, and as I drive in the first thing I notice is an old bloke with no hair holding court with the Grey Nomads in the pergola. He's the bush-poet-in-residence and he tells yarns, recites poems and plays the gumleaf. His audience is rapt, and I can see why: he has such an easy delivery style, there is no performance, so much as an entertaining bloke enjoying himself in company.

Nonetheless, I walk on by. That kind of obvious Australiana is not my thing.

The next morning as I'm checking out I notice a couple of his CDs for sale at reception, so I ask about him. I'm told he comes and stays for the winter as a guest of the proprietors, and assured he's a real 'character'.

Again, I keep walking. When people refer to someone as a 'character' I'm immediately wary. They're often referring to the obvious traits in their personality, or their Australian-ness, or even their blokeish-ness, none of which I find nearly so interesting as subtlety and depth of character. And despite my birthright I'll still choose humanity over nationality every day.

But as I'm packing up to leave I notice the old poet putting out the garbage. He isn't getting a lot done because he keeps getting held up for a chat by his fans, but he's all smiles and laughs and jokes, just like he was the day before.

So I change my mind and ask him if he'd chat with me for the radio. Of course he's happy to, and doesn't care where it's broadcast, it's enough to have a yak.

'I'm just an old bloke having a bit of fun before I get the plug pulled on me,' he tells me. 'I've been coming up here for four years now, and I just do a bit of fishin' and wander about the bush lookin' for ideas for poetry. And pull me weight where I can. I'm not a bludger, no fear.'

He's seventy-three years old and he comes from the coast, and he tells me his best friend is his surf ski.

'I can't ride the big waves anymore. Don't want to surf in anything I can't get myself out of if I fall off the ski. No good goin' around makin' work for someone else,' he says. 'But I'm countin' on ridin' an eight-foot wave when I'm eighty. That's me plan.'

He was a pastry cook by trade and he raised his kids on his own. He tells me the poetry grew out of telling the kids stories and rhymes in the car, to stop them falling asleep before they got home.

He's performed at Tamworth, and wryly lists one of his achievements as getting a score of five points from the Scrooge of Judges in the talent quest segment of a popular variety show on my old network some years ago.

I ask him if he has a plan of attack when he stands up to perform.

'No, I don't have to worry about it,' he says. 'It's different to goin' in a competition. I've seen blokes get stressed out, strainin' to remember their lines, kickin' garbage bins. I just let it come out of me scone.'

He gives me a taste of his poetry and plays a song or two on the gumleaf, and leaves me a little richer for the experience. His chosen genre may be growing old with its audience, but there'll always be a forum for a 'character' of his calibre.

God thought that all our heads should match
And though he took great care
Some were faulty, not up to scratch
So he covered them with hair.

Garry Lowe – Australian bush poet.

BOMBS AND BONES

According to anecdotal evidence, in World War II we bombed our own schoolkids with mustard gas.

At the time, the military was stockpiling supplies of mustard gas and phosgene gas (chemical warfare agents) in Darwin, Northern Territory, and Richmond, Queensland, to counter similar moves by the Japanese in Papua New Guinea. It wasn't the smartest wartime decision ever made for a number of reasons, not least because Richmond in particular could be very easily isolated with one well-placed bomb on the Macrossan Bridge at Charters Towers.

I find one of the old diggers still living in Richmond and ask him if mustard gas was ever used in anger in this country.

'Not used aggressively,' he tells me, 'but it was used in experiments, which were all very hush, hush. I know they bombed a stack of goats on an island off the coast.'

He speaks in a gruff voice he keeps rolling in between words. Even his laugh, which he uses often, blends in with the words so the overall effect is a continuous growl, like an old dog dreaming about bigger bones and slower cats.

'What about on humans?' I ask him.

'Never had bombs dropped on them directly, but they did drop some in the vicinity of a school in Innisfail, and they got some horrendous burns there. No-one knew very much about it.'

'So what does mustard gas do?'

'Mustard gas gives the most horrific burn you can ever imagine,' he says. 'And when I say gas it was more like oatmeal; if you can imagine a thick porridge, that's what it was like. If we ever got careless and dropped a bit on the ground – it might only be a spot as big as a match head – and walked on it in our big rubber-soled air force boots, next morning you had a burn on the sole of your foot as big as a fifty-cent piece. And it was deep.

'That's how severe the gas is,' he continues, 'Most of us got minor burns, some got major burns.'

'Any compensation?'

'As far as the government was concerned it didn't happen. There was no mustard gas.'

'Did anybody try it on?'

'We had one chap out at the camp here, whose respirator failed while we were disposing of the phosgene gas, and we had no medical-grade oxygen so we hit him with the welding-grade oxygen from the workshop, you know, and he recovered quite well. I think he had a go at recovery, but they reckoned he wasn't damaged enough to warrant anything.'

And I can just imagine this old digger and his mates dragging the oxy bottle over to their gasping mate and blasting him with the oxygen. Never mind the niceties, just get some air into the poor bugger.

'So what happened to the gas after the war?'

'We were told to get rid of it. The phosgene wasn't so difficult because the gas escaped harmlessly once the canister was opened, but the mustard gas was a different story. So we carted it a few kilometres away from camp and doused it with fuel, then fired incendiaries into it, under the theory that the fire would generate enough heat to burst the canisters and burn off the mustard gas as it escaped.

'Well, that didn't work,' he says. 'And eventually they dug a big hole with a backhoe and buried it somewhere out there with the dinosaurs.'

Which could be anywhere in these parts, since it used to be an inland sea where all sorts of dinosaurs lived and died. For the purists it was the Cretaceous period, about a hundred million years ago, and the region is rich in evidence of this time. Several near-complete skeletons have been found, some important enough to have been appropriated by museums in Brisbane and Harvard, USA, and others no less significant now housed in Richmond's own museum.

And it seems old bones are new again, and as country towns all look for a competitive edge to entice the tourist trade to their regions, Richmond has a beauty. They have a well-stocked museum and information centre, and you can even have a scratch around for a few bones yourself at the approved diggings, before setting off on the rest of the dinosaur trail through central Queensland. Just be careful you don't dig up a bomb.

But I like my bones with the meat still on, and in Richmond I find the only butcher I've encountered on this trip who fattens and butchers his own cattle.

'You won't find better meat anywhere in Richmond,' the jolly-faced butcher tells me. His, of course, is the only butchery in Richmond. But it's also the best fillet I've found so far.*

I also run into a horse-whisperer. That's not what he calls himself – he's happy with horse-breaker – but the way he speaks of horses makes me think otherwise.

'We don't like to do the rope and choke thing anymore,' he says. 'We use bigger yards so we don't have to invade their space so much.

'And I can usually get a hand on even the wildest within a couple of sessions. Just by letting them get used to you.'

He tells me for his fee he puts thirty rides on a horse, and he rates the American horsemen as the best he's seen, because there's so much more work over there, and more variety.

He's got a gentle manner and a thin, weathered face with pointed features, like he's spent all his life looking for signs, detail. He tells me he's forty-two years old and never had kids, but he's got a young girlfriend. I wish him luck with his breaking and move on.

I camp on the banks of the river, just to the north of the town. They've had a decent hit of rain over the past month and I set up overlooking a good, long waterhole and light a fire. It's a pretty stretch of country and I'm admiring the river gums and the sounds of the Australian bush when I notice the Prickly Acacia all around me.

Prickly Acacia is a weed of national significance introduced to Queensland from Pakistan in the early part of the last century. Some genius in the Department of Agriculture decided it would make an excellent shade tree and provide fodder for stock, despite the fact that it's covered in thorns so evil not even a cow is stupid enough to go near the thing, much less eat it. Now it's everywhere.

The next thing I see, just before dark, is a big ginger feral cat, standing about half a metre tall and watching me from about thirty metres away. He doesn't move or respond in any way to my coaxing, and bolts the instant I stand up.

Then, just as the darkness creeps in to meet the fire, I hear a rustling behind me. It sounds like a small rodent or marsupial of some kind, and I'm surprised to think a creature of its apparent size has managed to survive with a feral cat in the area. Then I see what's making the noise. It's a cane toad, hopping like a moron down to the river.

And right there, in the warmth of a eucalypt fire, I feel a little sad for my beautiful Australian bush.

* Didn't better it the whole trip. So I rang the butcher to congratulate him, and ask his secret: 'We fatten them on our own property just out of town,' he tells me, well pleased to receive my humble endorsement. 'So they're 100 per cent natural grass-fed Angus beef cattle – Mitchell and Flinders grasses we've got around here – and then we butcher them locally at about two and a half to three years old.'

'And that's it?'

'Yep. Oh, and always serve with a smile.'

NANNA AND THE SCYTHE

Somewhere in the backblocks of central Queensland I come across a vast junkyard for farm machinery. I've seen plenty of junkyards in my time, but never anything on a scale to match this one: it is enormous. And very colourful too, with acre upon acre of every imaginable piece of machinery ever used to till, plant, level, harvest, raze, bail, chop, scarify, pull, load, or any other farming verb you can name, painted in every imaginable colour, all assembled together in this great graveyard for retired farm equipment.

I wander around for about an hour just looking at the bits and pieces, some familiar to me, others a complete mystery, and I come across what looks like a motorised scythe without its wheels.

Now, for the record, the motorised scythe was perhaps the most cumbersome farm tool ever designed. It was basically a one-man harvester, with two long handles attached to a motor balanced between two large wheels, all driving a wide set of gnashing blades capable of mowing down anything in its path up to and including tree saplings.

It was too heavy to push, and the motor drove not only the blades but also the wheels. So when you started it up you had to be quick to engage the clutch or the bloody thing lurched into action and started chomping away at anything in its path. Similarly, when you were using it you had to get the clutch in and the beast swung around just before the end of the run, or you could easily find yourself impaled in a shed. Quite literally.

Indeed I remember a time ours ran amok and took out the aviary, and Nanna tried to kill it with her walking stick.

She'd been badgering Dan the Man and me to build this aviary for ages, to house all the parrots we had living in cages on the veranda of the farmhouse. She was sick of the mess they made, and the constant squawking.

'I've got my eyes on yooouuuu,' she'd tell the birds through the louvred windows.

Then she'd turn and berate us at the breakfast table.

'If you boys don't do something about those birds I'll feed them to the cats,' she'd say, and mean nothing of the sort. Then she'd give the closest of us a crack on the head with her walking stick to show she was serious.

It should be noted that Nanna was a fairly theatrical soul with a keen sense of humour, and when she hit one of us on the head with her stick it wasn't to hurt us, but more for the performance value. That said, sometimes her performances were more heartfelt than others and it was best to avoid the rap if you could.

Eventually we decided to build an aviary as much to get some peace as anything else.

There was no shortage of timber lying around the farm so material wasn't an issue, and working steadily through a fine spring day we had no trouble knocking together an aviary frame by mid-afternoon. We even gave it a fully-hinged door and a corrugated iron shelter. All we needed now was to cover the thing with chicken wire to complete the job.

As we sat admiring our efforts, Nanna came to inspect. She walked around the frame, then through it, all the while tapping this joint with her walking stick, then that one, as if the sound alone would reveal any flaws in our work.

Finally she made a big show of waving her stick where the wire netting had not yet been applied and said, 'They'll fly straight out of that.' Then she walked away with a smirk on her face.

But summer rushed in that year and soon there were school friends to entertain and swimming holes to explore and campouts to have, just too many diversions for young boys to handle and stay focused on the building of an aviary. The naked timber frame greyed in the sun. The grass grew long. Nanna grew irritated.

'If you boys don't mow that grass I'll catch the next snake I see and put it in your bed,' she said.

Of course we took no notice. But gradually she wore us down with cracks to the skull and eventually Dan consented to mow the grass in the house paddock, which was about waist high by this stage and well beyond the capabilities of a lawn mower, even if we did have one. No, this was a job for the motorised scythe.

Despite the scythe being a cumbersome brute of a thing, Dan was a strong lad even in early adolescence and he had no trouble handling it. At the end of each run he would engage the clutch and heave it around to face the other way, then release the clutch and set off again. It was part muscle, part timing, and just the kind of battle he enjoyed. The sun was warm on his back, and he was thinking about cooling off in the dam when he finished.

Then he heard the phone bell ring, so he engaged the clutch and ran for it. Ours was a poultry farm and the phone was left for us kids to answer on weekends when the farm was unattended. Usually it was a customer ringing for eggs, and it never took long to take an order.

It was, however, just long enough for the old scythe to rattle the clutch free and set off towards the aviary. It wasn't fast, but it was powerful, and it took out the first corner post in its stride. Then the beast twisted the whole frame into a splintery, corrugated tangle as it turned the aviary inside out.

By the time Dan returned, the scythe had demolished the aviary and was locked in battle with one of the house piers, blades gnashing and wheels axle deep in the loamy soil, with Nanna try to stop it by belting it with her walking stick and remonstrating:

'Get out of that, you stupid thing. Get out!'

NOT A COWBOY

Mount Isa 2007 – There's no more surreal place for a city slicker than a country rodeo.

To begin with it feels like you're on a western movie set, as if the organisers have paid actors to walk around in cowboy gear to give the show an authentic feel. They even call each other Cowboy, for Christ's sake! In time you realise most of these guys are for real: competitors, for instance, are fined if they're not in western gear, and many of the cowboys are ringers and farmhands who wear similar clothes on a daily basis. But your initial impression is likely to be one of scepticism.

And of course where there are cowboys there are bound to be cowgirls; and to see these fresh-faced angels peeking out from their upturned hats, sashaying around in their in their spray-on jeans and cowgirl boots, is to imagine you're in the middle of a beautiful dream directed by your best friend the devil. I couldn't care less if it's all for show and next week they revert to civvies for their office jobs, they're so damn cute I cricked my neck.

Then there's the fact that everybody drinks rum, and plenty of it; and that's about as close to surrealism in a can as you can get, whether you're drinking the evil potion or just watching the fallout.

And lastly let's not forget the entertainment, which usually involves putting an animal through some sort of activity that offends the sensibilities of the politically correct. If you approach a rodeo from a sensitive city perspective it will almost surely seem bizarre that people are still allowed to get away with this stuff.

My considered advice is to have another rum and go with it. Rodeos have been around for a long time; probably even before the Americans made them popular in the eighteenth- and nineteenth-century Wild West, and maybe even before the Spanish *vaqueros* introduced their cowboy skills and distinctive dress code to the Americans in the first place. It's just farm boys showing off for the girls: the oldest game in town. With animals.

For the record, I'm not a cowboy, though I have had a small taste of rodeo before. Bull riding, in fact; only not in the ring. When I was a teenager my cousin Dan and his mate flirted with the idea of going on the bull-riding circuit, so they dragged me along to help yard up the neighbour's cattle for riding practice. Naturally I got coerced into riding a few for their entertainment. So, however lowly my grade of entry, I do know the feeling of exhilaration associated with roping yourself to a large beast determined to throw you.

Of course the bulls used in modern day rodeos are in a different league; they're purpose-bred and stars in their own right, sometimes even bigger stars than the cowboys. They still talk in revered tones about a bull called Chainsaw, now long since hamburgered. At this meet a couple of the big names are Hard Yards and Lethal Injection, just to satisfy your burning curiosity.

I'm interested to see how much the bulls demeanour mimics that of the competing cowboys. Backstage at a bull riding competition is no different from the dressing rooms before any team sporting fixture. The cowboys walk around nervously, or sit quietly cross-checking gear or chewing tobacco, each one observing a ritual of preparation developed for an optimum state of readiness. And bugger me if the bulls don't look like they're doing exactly the same thing! I suggest this to one of the stock breeders who supply the animals.

'Oh, yeah,' he says. 'They know where they are and they know why they're here. They're athletes, same as the cowboys. You watch how quickly they get out of the ring once they've done their job.'

I do, and he was right, however long the bow he was drawing.

With one or two exceptions the bulls all head straight for the exit once they've bucked off their rider and his rope. If nothing else they know the drill.

I prefer the bulls to the broncs. With bulls, the rider has to sit upright and there's a real sense of symmetry, and an aesthetically obvious meeting point between man and beast. With the broncs, the current trend seems to be for the cowboy to lay right back along the horse's spine, so for much of the time it looks more like he's flapping than riding.

My favourite, though, is the wild horse race. This event is so action-packed and unpredictable you need more than one pair of eyes to take it all in. The basic concept is for teams of three cowboys to each control an unbroken brumby long enough to throw a saddle and rider on its back and get it across a finish line. It's pandemonium. You've got horses bucking saddles off, men flying through the air or getting dragged along the ground, horses biting cowboys and, wait for it, cowboys biting horses. Seriously. And they do this not out of cruelty, but because this is how the alpha horse in any herd imposes it's superiority over the rest. So in the midst of the chaos, if you see one horse standing quietly while the saddle is being fixed and the rider legged up, look closely and you'll almost certainly see a cowboy clamped to the horse's ear.

This is the first year in the new arena for the rodeo and everything seems to be running smoothly. Without fuss the stock are selected, chuted, mounted and set loose in the ring for what the announcer calls, 'Eight seconds of pure hell.'

That's a long time to cling to a tonne of beast and the crowd grows more vocal with every second, urging the cowboy on. If he makes time on a well-performing bull, the cowboy usually tosses his hat in the air to the delight of the crowd, assuming of course he's managed a stylish dismount. It's a gesture not nearly so impressive from a sitting position – funnier perhaps, but cowboys aren't known for their humour in the ring, only their bravado.

The humour they leave to the clowns, who need two skills to do their job: humour for the crowd and courage for the cowboy. These days we're supposed to call them intervention technicians or interference cowboys or some other politically correct nonsense, but they'll always be clowns to me. I've never doubted the importance of the job, on any stage.

And back in the grounds the cowgirls captivate and the party rages and the action starts early and finishes late. It's not the wildest show I've ever been to, but it's getting close to the most bizarre.

LAST MAN STANDING

His silver hair looks like it's been electric-shocked. The royal blue satin shirt he's wearing looks like it's been pulled from his pocket. His face is flushed and his voice is shot. Yet when he climbs up on his platform and starts banging his drum and spruiking the crowd he is every bit the showman.

'Ladies and gentlemen gather round. Fresh from the length and breadth of Australia exceptin' the backward states of New South Wales and Victoria – we got anyone from those states here tonight? You? And you there, sir? Welcome to Australia – from every outback town and country fair I present to you the world-famous boxin' tent that's been in me family for four generations and is surely the last one of its kind left in Australia, if not the world, right here at the Mount Isa Rodeo. Let's have a rally on the drums and bells.'

And he bangs the drum with a tried and tested rhythm and one of his boxers standing up the far end of the platform rings the bell and the crowd gathers. It's a sound so arresting it will draw you in from anywhere in the arena, and when you arrive at the tent with the boxers painted on the facade you will truly think you've gone back in time. It's a sight so vaudeville you wouldn't be surprised to see the half-man, half-woman appear from within the tent and take its place on the scaffolding stage before you.

'Ladies and gentlemen,' he continues, 'allow me to introduce you to my troupe of dedicated boxers. At the far end, that old, short bloke there may not look like much but he's never been defeated. Ladies and gentlemen, please welcome The Birdsville Mauler. Let's give him a rally.'

And then comes another round on the bells and drums, followed by another introduction and another rally, until the entire troupe has been introduced and it's time to start plucking contenders from the crowd.

'So who's the best fighter out here tonight? Where's that bloke with the big mouth? Come on all you young blokes, better off gettin' it out of your system here where we can keep an eye on you, than over in the bar later. What about you there? That young fella there with the long hair. Come on up here. That's good.'

And they get up: boys of every size, shape and colour. They are ringers and plumbers and cowboys and drunks – though not too drunk they can't walk along the narrow platform stage to prove their sobriety. Some are dared by their mates or come up with them; others do it on impulse, finessed by the cajoling man with the drum. Yet another young bloke I spoke to did it because his father had done it years ago and told him to do it now before it's gone forever. And they all climb the ladder and walk the plank to face the crowd.

'And what's your name, young fella?' the boss asks, never relinquishing the microphone for a second for the crowd to hear the kid's answer. 'Ever done any boxing in the ring before? No? So you're undefeated, then. What about on the streets? A bit. Can't help 'emselves, some of these young blokes. Righto, you can have The Italian Stallion there. You can fight him. Now move along the plank a bit. And what's your name?'

And when the lads are all matched with boxers, they file into the tent, followed by the crowd, which brings with it the noise of expectation.

The floor is bark chips and in the centre is a vinyl mat with a bench at either end. There are about twenty plastic chairs scattered around what could loosely be termed ringside, but once these are filled people sit, stand and crouch, until the tent is full of people and the sound and smell of sport.

The contenders are stripped to the waist, hands gloved and eye–brows greased, and get their pep talk from a designated handler.

'Don't worry too much about boxing,' he says. 'Leave that to the real boxers. Just keep your gloves up and get the feel of your man for a bit, then take your shots when you can.'

One of the boys is a ringer from one of the stations hereabouts. He's about eighteen years old and owns a mop of curly blonde hair. He's no thicker than a pencil, but wiry, like he's not afraid of hard work, and he's at the rodeo to ride the broncs. I ask him what his plan of attack is.

'Go hard or go home, I reckon,' he tells me.

He's tag teaming with his mate who's also a bronc rider and about the same size and weight, but not as talkative.

'Reckon I'll be too busy,' his mate tells me when I ask him if he minds me sticking a microphone in his face between rounds. Fair enough.

Meanwhile the boxers in the troupe are loosening up and disrobing and donning gloves and grease, and pretty soon all four fighters in the match are in the middle with the boss getting their rights read.

'We fight by Queensbury rules here, no punching below the

belt, biting or gouging, if a boxer goes off the mat you let him back on before you continue, you have to win to get the money and if I think you're getting hurt I'll stop the fight. Shake hands.'

Then he blows his whistle and it's on. The skinny kids follow their plan and go hard and get a few punches on the professionals. They tag each other when they knock up or start getting knocked about, and the better the kids go, the more the crowd loves it. There's not a lot of style about them, but plenty of pluck.

I'm switching my focus from the fight to the crowd, watching the women in particular. They don't show a lot of emotion but you can see they're hooked. I ask a young woman of about twenty-five what the attraction is.

'Just watching blokes belt each other,' she says, not taking her eyes off the fighting for a second. 'Doesn't get any better than that.'

It's primal stuff, no doubt, harking back to a time when a man had to fight for survival, and if he couldn't fight he didn't breed. These days it's money that calls the shots, but it's comforting to know that basic instinct still lives.

The three rounds are over all too quickly and the crowd shows its appreciation. The young bronc riders don't get the decision but they earn plenty of respect. I ask The Birdsville Mauler what he thought of the boys.

'Yeah, they went well, didn't they?' he says, still catching his breath. 'We need more kids like that. Good kids, prepared to step up and make men of themselves. It's good to see.'

The next day I visit the tent and talk to the boxers. The Birdsville Mauler is forty-four and reckons he'll carry on till he's fifty. The star turn of the troupe, Cowboy, could have forged a decent career in the ring, but prefers the tent circuit because it's more casual and he can still run his concreting business back home. They're from all over the state and they join the tent whenever they can fit it in around work. They're just normal guys with normal jobs, who just happen to be handy enough with their fists to make a bit of extra pocket money when it's show time.

The boss is in a circumspect mood. I ask him how long he thinks he'll keep the tent going and he says this might be his last year. He wants to retire and write a book. I'm told later that he's been threatening to retire for years, but right now he looks like he's ready.

I ask him if there's anyone left to run the tent after he's gone.

'No, mate,' he tells me. 'I'm the last one, I reckon.'

And then he looks at me for a long moment and says nothing.

THE INTERVENTION

On the strength of a report written by Rex Wild and Pat Anderson about the state of Aboriginal communities in the Northern Territory, the federal government decided to spend nearly six hundred million dollars on what it called an Emergency Response Intervention Program to fix the deteriorating health and social problems highlighted in the report.

My assignment for this leg of the journey is to see how this Intervention Program's task force is travelling – the lead group made up of health, welfare, army and logistics personnel responsible for initiating the 'roll out' – and my intention is to visit a few communities to gauge the people's response.

I know the task force started in the south, so I drive out to Hermannsburg, west of Alice Springs, to see how they're faring.

Hermannsburg was the first Aboriginal Mission in the Territory and was founded by the Lutherans in 1877. The Immanuel Synod of South Australia took over in 1891, but it still operated as an industrious and nearly self-sufficient church mission until 1982, when the Aboriginal Land Rights Act handed control back to the traditional owners, the Arrernte people.

Although the work sirens still sound, since that time Hermannsburg has gradually reverted to a more traditional style of Aboriginal community. Sadly, in the process it has developed many of the symptoms of a society in chaos, such as alcohol and substance abuse, domestic violence, insufficient and inadequate housing, poor standard of health and education, along with the main emphasis of the aforementioned report, child neglect and abuse, particularly sexual abuse.

I stayed for two days and two nights, and bearing in mind it was off-pay week so the influence of alcohol was always going to be minimal, in summary this is what I saw:

- No gardens, many dogs, rubbish everywhere.
- Happy, healthy-looking kids playing, when they should have been at school.
- Young men, black and white, renovating a burnt-out home.
- Women running an art gallery and childcare facility.
- Two sporting club houses built and subsequently trashed by the young men.
- Other young men embarrassed to admit to a community child-abuse problem.
- People suspicious and concerned about the Intervention Program (IP).
- Local police unwilling to comment on the IP.
- Local councillors unclear about the implications of the IP.
- A new office block built by outside contractors to house the IP administrators.
- Frustration at the lack of consultation with the community regarding the IP.
- General despair that the funding for the IP was going to be wasted.
- A flock of Major Mitchell Cockatoos, for the first time in my

life.

I head up 'the track' feeling totally out of my depth, and hoping Hermannsburg is an isolated example.

'The track' in Territory-speak is the Stuart Highway, the main road extending almost eighteen hundred kilometres from the South Australian border to Darwin.

I travel slowly, stopping to talk to anyone who might have an opinion about the IP. Some have no idea what I'm talking about, but the majority do, and the overwhelming response is confusion and fear. They are afraid of what will happen to their welfare payments and the work-for-pay scheme (the Community Development Employment Program, or CDEP), and they don't understand why the government wants to remove the permit system and take a leasehold over their land.

There's nothing surprising in these responses, of course – none of us are fond of change – any more than I'm surprised by the scepticism of the community workers charged with the responsibility of explaining the IP to their communities.

What is interesting, though, is the strong support for the IP in the towns, far removed from the communities themselves. I hope it isn't just a 'guilt-driven response'; in other words, 'As long as I believe something is being done I can keep my own conscience clear, but if I look too closely and discover problems I'll have to remain guilty.' There's no equality in guilt, whichever way you look at it.

I camp at Mataranka Hot Springs and go for a 2 am dip in one of the thermal pools. It's a good time to do it if you want to avoid the crowds. And don't be alarmed by the noises in the bush: they're just Agile Wallabies not living up to their name. The path is easy enough to follow, even on a moonless night, and when you get to the pool you'll have it all to yourself. The water's a gentle warm, and when you float on your back it feels like you're in the

Above: *Darling River, May 2007, Wilcannia, New South Wales – story page 11.*

Below: *Darling River, March 2008, Wilcannia, New South Wales.*

Above: *Soft as a cloud, cotton country, southern Queensland – story page 18.*

Below: *The Painted Hills, Anna Creek Station, South Australia – story page 152.*

Above: *Aboriginal rock art, Injalak, Arnhem Land, Northern Territory – story page 101.*

Below: *Rural road art, anywheresville, central Queensland.*

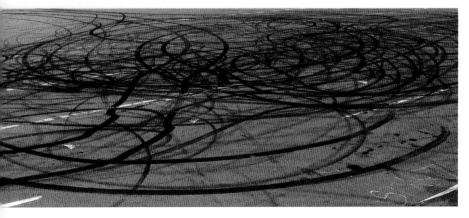

LEGEND

- ———— THE TRIP
- ▦ GREAT ARTESIAN BASIN
- – – – – STATE BORDERS
- ———— RIVERS
- ∿∿∿ GREAT BARRIER REEF

ARUF
SE

TIMOR SEA

JOSEPH
BONAPARTE Darwin
GULF

BROWSE
BASIN

Wyndham
Kununurra

THE
KIMBERLEY

Broome

Fitzroy
Crossing
Halls Creek
Wolfe Creek

GREAT SANDY DESERT

NORT

PINNACLE
DESERT

Rabbit Flat

Port Headland

Dampier

Cloud Break

Newman

GIBSON DESERT

TERRA

North West Cape

THE
PILBARA

WESTERN

Shark Bay
Denham

AUSTRALIA

GREAT VICTORIA DESERT

SO

Kalbarri

Meekatharra

AUS

Geraldton

Kalgoorlie

NULLARBOR PLAIN

INDIAN
OCEAN

Lancelin

Perth

Balladonia

Mandurah
Collie

Esperance

GREAT AUSTRALIAN BIGHT

Augusta

Albany

THE STATS

Vehicle	Hymer Happy Tramper (The Parrot)
Distance	70,000 kms (approx.)
Time	10 months (approx.)
Fuel consumption	No idea
Breakdowns	3 (all self-inflicted)
Flat tyres	5 (all on the bottom)
Accidents	Major – none; Minor – give me a break!
Demerit points lost	No comment

Disclaimer - this map is
representative only; if you
try using it as a travel guide
you'll end up as lost as I did!

Above: *The cap tree, via Renmark, South Australia.*

Below: *The undecided tree, can't remember, Queensland.*

Above: *The red dirt, Pilbara, Western Australia – story page 123.*

Below: *The angle pole, Oodnadatta Track, South Australia – story Page 152.*

The ANGLE POLE memorial

UHF CH.

On the Oodnadatta Track 7 kms sth. of Oodnadatta

The 1872 Overland Telegraph Line (OTL) was that centuries great technical feat, allowing 'morse' conversation between London & Sydney. It' little wire on pine posts, change direction at this point moving north at an angle towards Bloods Ck. The 'angle pole' waterhole nearby on 'Todmorden' cattle station was so important that the first section of rail built by 1891 was called 'The Port Augusta & Angle Pole Railway'. This area was a support base before the rail or Oodnadatta were built. The rail line ran close to the OTL here & this post would have been abandoned when OTL crews swapped horses for rail cars for maintenance runs (ceramic insulators were popular targets for locals practising rock throwing skills)

1874 explorer John Forrest arrived at this point, desperate after a difficult journey from W.A. across the desert, the future W.A. State Premier blazed a tree which became a monument at Angle Pole waterhole (see 'Horrie Simpsons' Oodnadatta 'book for photo.) He followed the OTL south to 'Peake' which was the most northerly town in SA. Recently at the waterhole, local historians & camel tour operators, Phil & Ifeta Gee saw a legendary NIGHT PARROT there! The hills here have been dug a bit over the years for road base, rail repairs & possibly paint pigment. Go Walking – but dont drive or remove articles please!
* DONT CAMP AT ANGLE POLE WATERHOLE.

PINK ROADHOUSE 2005

The yellow dog, central Queensland – story page 136.

world's most exotic bathroom, with Livistonia Palm walls and a ceiling of incomparable starry beauty.

For a blast of near-absolute peace, exhale and let your body sink to the bottom. You'll probably only manage to stay under for twenty or thirty seconds, but for that time you'll hear almost nothing. Makes you realise how noisy the world can be.

In the morning I tackle the Wild/Anderson *Little Children Are Sacred* report: a harrowing read by any standards. And while it contains nothing new for people who've worked in Aboriginal health – which, for the record, I have – the magnitude of the problem suggested a serious deterioration in Aboriginal living standards since I worked as a nurse in the Territory back in the early eighties.

The federal government's proposed 'broad and sweeping changes' had its supporters, but at least one of the report's authors had publicly criticised the response, and there were many critics less prepared to go public among the health professionals I still knew in the Territory.

'There was just no real consultation,' said one highly-ranked ex-colleague of mine. 'Not with us, not with any of the government departments, and worst of all not with the communities themselves, either with the administration or the elders.

'Basic human rights issues aside, do we really think we can 'normalise' these people? And what's normal anyway? Cronulla? Aurukun?

'And here we go again wasting more money on short-term, politically motivated solutions, duplicating health data we already had, discovering Aboriginal kids have got ear problems, eye problems, diabetes; we already knew all that stuff! We could have put an extra health worker in every community for a year for the cost of that exercise.'

Then he just shook his head and smiled a helpless smile by way of conclusion.

In order to connect to the internet and download the report I have the laptop sitting on a wheelie bin in the caravan park, and in the process a man with his bare belly hanging over his shorts passes me and delivers the following witticism:

'Found the right place for that thing, mate,' he says, indicating the laptop.

'How's that?' I ask.

'In the garbage bin,' he says.

In light of what I'm reading, I find his joke mildly objectionable. Just goes to show how sobering this stuff is, I guess.

I decide I'm growing uncharitable and need a walk, so I wander downstream aways and come across a Dutch backpacker sitting on her own at a waterhole. She tells me she's working at a nearby cattle station and, while she didn't much like her boss, she enjoyed the work. Back in Holland she'd been a secretary, and looking after distressed calves and fencing and other station duties was exotic and exciting for her. Though she didn't enjoy having to help her boss cut up for dog meat the calf whose life they'd been trying to save.

'I cannot be present for this bullshit cruelty,' she says, speaking with an entertaining mix of studied formality and newly adopted slang. 'And he is raising his voice at me, very impolite, but I tell him to shove his job if I am required to do this.'

She is twenty-six years old and says she loves Australia, and is working at the cattle station in order to qualify for a visa extension.

When I tell her she is welcome she smiles like it's the nicest thing anyone has ever said to her.

We are sitting in the shade of the Melaleuca trees that line the streams hereabouts, and she tells me she hasn't seen a crocodile in the three months she's been in the Territory. I tell her there are plenty of big ones to see and she promises to make the effort to see one before she leaves. She asks me what I'm doing and, when I tell her, she's surprised I have such a positive take on Aborigines.

'People tell me they are no good,' she says, 'that they are lazy and get drunk all the time, and only wait for the government money to get more drink.'

I'd been so immersed in looking at the issue from a work perspective I'd forgotten this was the default opinion of many Australians.

'Sure, some are,' I say. 'But they're not all like that. Without the grog they're an entirely different proposition.'

So we talk a bit about the problems facing our Aborigines and I tell her there are plenty of good ones to know and she promises to make the effort to know one before she leaves.

Then I leave her to the rest of her adventure and get back to mine.

The next morning I cross to Charlie and deliver the (mostly) bad news I'm hearing about the response to the Intervention Program, and he recommends I get in touch with the Major General in charge of the task force for his point of view.*

I also ring the federal minister's office and ask one of his staffers why the minister seems to be ignoring the recommendations proposed in the report, the same report the federal government was citing as its motivation for the Intervention.

'Because the minister saw a disconnection between the content of the report and the recommendations,' I'm told. 'Specifically that there was no mention of increasing police presence in these communities to protect the little children.'

Now I have to say that isn't quite my take on the report, so I bring it up with Territory's then Chief Minister, Clare Martin, when I meet with her later that week.

'Fred Chaney was quoted in the [Wild/Anderson] report,' I say, 'as saying if there's one thing we should have learned by now it is that we cannot resolve these issues from any bureaucratic position in Canberra, and that it must be done on the ground at the source of the problems. Why do you think the federal government seems to be ignoring his advice?'

'Again I go back to my view of Minister Brough,' she replies, 'who takes very much the view that "there is an answer here, and I can find it, and I can implement it, and I can do it in a very short timeframe". In that, Minister Brough is wrong. And I would certainly advise – I mean Fred Chaney is held with great respect in Liberal circles and I would certainly advise Mal Brough to go and have a chat with Fred.'

'Do you think he's read the report?'

'The last information I had from Minister Brough, which was in the federal Parliament, was that he hadn't read the report. And he also told me over the table that, "No I haven't read the report. But I don't like its recommendations so I'm going to act unilaterally."'**

* Before the Major General would agree to an interview I had to reveal my line of questioning, which included the concerns raised above. Then he declined my request.

** Minister Brough went on to lose his seat in the federal election, and shortly thereafter Clare Martin resigned from her role as Chief Minister. Brough could certainly claim his demise was more due to a national swing against his party than the Intervention Program, but I think it's fair to say the reputations of both politicians were tarnished by the affair.

TRADITIONAL COMPROMISES

Gunbalunya is called Oenpelli because Leichhardt the explorer misread the field notes when it came time to compile them. It says something about the locals that they don't care what you call their home as long as you respect it. I lived in the Territory for ten years or so and this is my first visit: that's how strong a disincentive permit protection can be. Unless you had a work-related cause to go, or an interest compelling enough to make you go through the rigmarole of getting a permit, you left it alone. With the Intervention Program involving the removal of the permit system, places like Gunbalunya, situated so close to Kakadu National Park, would likely be impacted greatly.*

Especially since it's surely one of the prettiest short drives in the country, from Cahill's Crossing at the East Alligator River to the community a further twenty kilometres or so along the sandstone escarpment. And when you reach the town itself the view is even more spectacular. Along with the usual jumble of houses and car wrecks and camp dogs, you're greeted by a majestic chunk of the escarpment jutting up from a vast lagoon stocked shore-to-shore with all manner of Territory wildlife.

I'm told it has the highest biomass quotient in the world, or more bugs, plants and animals per cubic metre than anywhere else on the planet.

Of an afternoon you'll often see great flocks of Black Kites and pelicans soaring to heights of two hundred metres or more on the thermal currents around the lagoon: birds flying for the sheer pleasure of being alive.

Apart from taking a look at the obvious issue, I'm also looking to do a colour piece for the radio to show it's not all doom and gloom on the communities. Charlie suggests I go on a goanna hunt, but the arrival of the cane toad in the Top End has had an adverse affect on goanna numbers and they're now few and far between.

I choose to go fishing for barramundi instead: with spears.

Nobody uses spears much any more – sensibly, they prefer rifles – but eventually I track down a bloke who looks like Omar Sharif who's happy to take me on a traditional fishing expedition. Only problem is he's got no spears, so we have to borrow some from the Injalak Art Centre, one of the real success stories in community art centres in the Territory. The spears are heavily decorated and were probably intended for sale as artefacts rather than as hunting weapons, and we're loaned them on the proviso that we promise to bring them back.

I ask Omar if he's sure he can throw a spear.

'Sure I can,' he tells me. 'I'm a blackfella.'

We're being joined on the hunt by the local Land Management Ranger, so the crew is two whitefellas, neither of whom have ever thrown a spear, and Omar, who could easily be having a lend of me. Naturally we embark brimful of confidence: the *numungul* (barramundi) don't stand a chance.

'What about crocodiles?' I ask Omar.

'Plenty *ginga*,' he says.

'*Ginga*, you call 'em? So who goes in to fetch the spears we throw?'

'Not me,' says Omar. 'Maybe the ranger will.'

'No way, mate,' says the ranger. 'It's your country.'

But Omar's having none of it. He originally hails from north-east Arnhem Land so he's quick to disown this western Arnhem country if it means he's responsible for fetching the spears.

And so the banter flows, and continues when we reach the billabong, with nobody game to throw a spear for fear of having to go in the water to retrieve it. Various theories are put forward about how we can explain a missing spear, and Omar suggests we tell the Arts Centre we speared a pig but it kept running. In the end we decide we're better off taking the spears back and returning with a cast net, which is what we do.

So the traditional hunting trip is rounded off with me wading out into the *ginga*-infested billabong to throw the cast net – I'm nominated because Omar assures me he can't use one, though he could be pulling my leg about this too – over a mixed haul of barra, mullet, sleepy cod, catfish, and the jewel in the crown, a Short-necked Turtle; all doubtless destined for a traditional end.

And while it's hard to pin down exactly where the cultural exchange was in that lot – perhaps it was in the shared laughter – it's probably a fair, albeit left-field, example of the complex nature of the interface between our two cultures today.

Another example was presented to me earlier, when one of the traditional owners agreed to talk to me about how the Intervention Program was likely to affect his community. I was to meet him at the community's 'wet' club, which is open at lunchtime for a couple of hours, but only serves mid-strength beer.

So he suggested we go somewhere quieter, somewhere like Jabiru, for instance, where we could get some full-strength beers while we were at it. And I really didn't know what to think: driving one of the elders into town to get some beers, in order to get him to talk about the dangers of alcohol abuse, et al, in his community.

Another of the elders told me he lamented losing the power of traditional punishments for crimes such as domestic violence and child sex abuse.

'In tribal ways,' he told me, 'customary laws meant violence was handled by the family of whoever did it; like a young man to a young woman, the two families used to deal with that, right across the board, starting from west Arnhem to east.

'But in western Arnhem Land,' he continued, 'they usually just downed the man without having any further meeting if he did child abuses. Simple as that.

'Kill him?'

'Yep. They just got rid of him. Because he was no good for the rest of the years, so no place was left for him. But nowadays, the government law means if you punish the man, you end up in jail.

'I've heard a few stories about guys who did that, to a young girl, and they go to jail, and they're now out and back to square one. They may be quiet for a while, even maybe now, but what they've done in the past, it's still in their mind.'

Before I leave Gunbalunya, Omar takes me for a walk up to the top of the escarpment and shows me the burial grounds and the rock art. We sit together for quite a while taking in the view overlooking the billabong and the community. I feel at one with my brother in his land.

Then he asks me for a lift to Darwin and fifty bucks for his trouble.

* The incoming federal Labor government abolished this element of the IP and returned the permit system.

TABLE OF MEMORIES

I have friends in Darwin who are heavily into the fine art of entertaining. They've been doing it for as long as I've known them; now they run a popular bed-and-breakfast joint on the outskirts of town and come sundown it's almost expected of them to join their guests for a drink outside. At least that's their story.

So on any given night through the dry season at the table under the stars, you're likely to find people of all colours, compass points and contemplations sharing the stuff that brings us all together.

It's heady living, not to mention addictive, and it all happens at the dining table of my friends.

A jovial puppeteer joins us. He and his wife have been travelling the country in a campervan for a number of years. She's a health professional who works locums in country hospitals where they arise. He lines up puppet workshops in schools wherever they go. I ask him what started him on such an off-beat career path.

'I grew up in England,' he tells me, 'so Punch and Judy was a very big influence, as were the Muppets and Jim Henson; learning that he ripped his mother's coat apart to make a frog inspired me.'

'Tell me about that.'

'Yeah, I'm not sure how old he was, but he had an idea, and he went and got his mum's green coat, and he cut it up and turned it into the original Kermit the Frog.

'So the Muppets – or *Sesame Street*, which is still going – was a big influence. As was *The Thunderbirds*, and *Star Wars* – the original Yoda was a puppet. They computer-generated him in all the sequels, but in the original he was puppetry, operated by Jim Hensen.'

'How big can you go with a puppet?'

'Oh, as big as you like. Last year in London they had an elephant walking through the streets, and he was forty-two tonnes. Called The Sultan's Elephant and built by some crazy French people.'

'How small?'

'Well I don't think there's nano-puppetry yet, but very small shadow figures, finger puppets... and I know in New York recently they held a puppet festival, and the smallest show was in a public toilet and played to an audience of one. The puppeteer sat on the toilet to perform the show and you had to sign a secrecy agreement so you didn't tell anybody else what it was about. So puppets can be as large or small or weird as you like.'

A naturalist and a biologist from America are guests while they tour the Top End photographing wildlife, and they've set up a tent in the grounds to photograph bats. I ask them how they plan to make the bats pose for the camera.

'Well, we make them fly through a flight chamber,' the biologist says, 'which is basically a long box with one end closed, and when they fly out through the open end they trigger an electronic shutter on the camera and take their own picture.'

He shows me some pictures he's taken of the bats flying as if through the outer foliage of a gum tree. I compliment him on the clarity of the shot, then accuse him of faking it. Rather than taking offence at the accusation he's well pleased.

'But it looks natural, doesn't it? It's what we call a fake naturescape. We put leaves and stuff at the mouth of the chamber so the bat looks like it's flying through the forest. If you've ever watched nature programs on the television with bat photography, those are all fake too, for the most part.'

At the table the naturalist entertains us with animal stories. He tells us that to get his teenage daughter to move out of the family computer room she'd taken over, he fumigated the room for Bark Scorpions (small and insignificant) and spread several dead Emperor Scorpions (large and terrifying) around the walls for her to discover. Years later he told her of the gag and she wouldn't believe him.

He also tells us of an alligator that has learned to swim upside down to hunt for turtles on the bottom of his pond – when he sights one he rolls over and dives down to catch it, before returning to the surface to toss it, crunch it and swallow it. Then he turns upside down again and starts looking for more turtles.

Just like a Spitfire pilot in World War II had to turn his plane upside down to eject from the cockpit. I'm told this by a man whose father had to ditch his aircraft on his way back from repelling a Japanese air raid on Darwin in 1943.

'People don't think twice about jumping out of a plane these days,' he tells me, 'they do it for fun. But back then it wasn't exactly common practice, and there was no good way to jump out of a spitfire except turn it on its back and drop out. Which is fine in theory, but when you haven't had practice and the engine's dead it's a rather difficult thing to do. But he managed it; he made it.

'Said it was the most wonderful experience of his life, watching that chute open and floating down as he watched the plane dive vertically into the sea.

'Then he landed in the water and he had his little inflatable dinghy, which came with two table-tennis bats for paddles, and he had about eighteen kilometres to paddle to reach the coast. It took him six hours, and he was accompanied for five of the six hours by a three-metre shark that never surfaced, he said, but was never more than about three metres away and scared the hell out of him.

'Then when he landed on the shore he realised it was unlikely anyone would know where to come looking for him, so he decided to walk back to base. It was about a hundred miles, he was young and fit, figured he'd head east for four days' hard slog. "Piece of cake" or so he thought. So he set off walking through the mangrove swamps.'

'He had no experience with the Top End at all. He said they'd talked a bit about crocs and mangroves and what-have-you in the briefing, but he thought, "I'm a pilot; I don't need to pay any attention to that."

'So he kept fighting his way through these swamps, which were getting deeper and deeper, some of them well over his head. And he was crossing a lot of creeks, but only small ones, about three or four metres wide. Runnels, he called them. It wasn't till about day five he came across one that was about two hundred metres wide.'

'Uh oh.'

'Indeed. As he said, no Territorian in their right mind would cross the thing, but he was pretty naive, so in he went. And he got about a third of the way across when he looked up and saw a destroyer-sized croc swimming towards him at full pace, he describes the water coming up around its snout, he describes the V-wave, and he thought, 'What a way to die.'

'Look I won't spoil the story for those who want to read it,* but he does get out of that.'

'So where was he sleeping?'

'He didn't.'

'The midges and mosquitoes must have eaten him alive.'

'They did. He tried submersing himself in water and breathing through a straw – all the things you see on bad survivor shows – he buried himself in mud, but that had other things in it that were as bad as the sandflies. He basically didn't sleep at all for the first five days.'

'What did he eat?'

'The only thing he had to eat was on about day eight, I think, when he stepped on the back of Australia's unluckiest goanna, he said. In his words he murdered the poor devil and he and the flies ate what they could. And he did have a few ibis eggs of dubious quality later on.'

And back at the table of memories we are sharing another meal of excellent quality. My friends are in good spirit, or perhaps the other way around, and no doubt soon the stories will start; the stories of our lives, which are, after all, about the only original contributions any of us ever bring to the table.

* *Caterpillar Club Survivor* by Ross Smith Stagg.

BIG CROCS AND BOABS

My last port of call in the Territory is a working cattle station out near the western border.

From the highway the homestead is a long drive on a dirt road, but not an unpleasant one. It's boab country out here and they're an eye-catching tree, with their grotesque bottle shapes and glossy sheen. It's also escarpment terrain, so I'm escorted all the way by great runs of sandstone protrusions and sheer rock faces coloured ochre and yellow and cream.

Every so often a wallaby scoots across the road in front of me, Red-tailed Black Cockatoos sit defiantly in small trees lining the road, a goshawk carrying a snake wings through an opening in the bush, and a bolting emu ducks its long neck under an overhanging branch, creating for an instant the absurd impression of a headless scrub-runner. I enjoy the drive immensely.

The only minor glitch comes when I bottom out driving through a river gully and rip the tailpipe loose from its mountings. Unbeknown to me at the time, this triggers a series of problems and *The Parrot* is never the same again; but more on that later.

While very much a working cattle station, the owners have extended the infrastructure to accommodate tourism, and offer horseriding, fishing and hunting as options for their guests, along with experiencing all the workaday activities you'd expect of a cattle station.

This is also big river country, and where there's a big river in northern Australia you'll find big crocodiles. My host tells me they lose about three hundred cattle a year to crocs.

One solution they've proposed is to cull the old males by selective hunting, or sustainable harvesting, to use the more politically correct term. There's no shortage of rich trophy hunters around the world who'll pay big money to bag one, and if managed well it could be a win-win situation for everyone.

'I think people are still labouring under the misconception that to save an endangered species it's best to leave it alone,' my host tells me. 'But in this day and age the best way to ensure an animal's survival is to give it a monetary value, and make its habitat more valuable in its natural state than it would be developed.

'Around the world it's not the managed animals that are in trouble,' she continues, 'but the ones we've insisted on leaving to fend for themselves. And I defy anyone to tell me a well-placed bullet isn't a kinder way to go than the death that awaits an old crocodile in the wild.

'As the law stands, we can get approval to cull a certain number of crocs each year, but not through hunting. So if it's all the same to the crocs why not look at the issue unemotionally and welcome the benefit to tourism?'

My host also tells me a story about cannibalism among Top End aborigines, which was apparently a common practice for some tribes. Apparently they only considered the bones sacred, not the flesh, so it was no big deal to hungi the newly deceased and eat the body, before the bones were transported to the burial grounds and 'sorry business' was respectfully carried out. But they never ate the old or the infirm, only the young killed by misadventure or in battle. One man even told my source they always sent the fat boys into battle first because they made the best eating.

The only other guests at the station are a couple from Bath. They are the epitome of British politeness, and good company besides. He is an ex-army chap and tells me a yarn about a pet puma his regiment had during one of his postings.

'Remarkable creatures, pumas. Never seen one so agile,' he starts.

'The officer's mess tent had a billiard table, of course,' he continues, fully aware of the absurdity of the statement, 'and no matter how we arranged the balls, when the puma's handler got him to jump up onto the table he never once touched a ball. Just rearranged his feet mid-air and missed everything.'

He reminds me of the puma, himself, somehow managing to remain neat and clean at all times against all odds in the Australian outback. On the first morning he arrived alone for breakfast dressed in khaki shorts and shirt, complete with long socks and shoes, looking like a boy scout on his way to a jamboree.

That day we fished for barramundi on a muddy riverbank, and somehow I ended up looking like a total grub while he still looked clean and fresh. Didn't even get his shoes muddy. Even by late that afternoon, when he was posing with the wild boar he'd just shot, he was the portrait of neat: not a crease, not a mark, not a hair out of place. Remarkable creatures, Englishmen. Never seen one so tidy.

THE GREAT WET HOPE

The first thing that happened when I crossed into Western Australia was the confiscation of all my fruit and vegetables by another smirking quarantine official. (So, come on, what's the joke? Has word got around that I'm a repeat offender?)

The reason quarantine is so strict approaching Kununurra is its proximity to the Ord River Scheme, an irrigation initiative begun in the 1960s by damming the river to create Lake Kununurra, and bolstered during the following decade by creating Lake Argyle as a storage facility.

Last time I came this way I went out to the lake. It was on a 1990 trip from Darwin to Perth. Here's what I said about it then:

Lake Argyle hasn't seen good rain for three years. The local catch is Silver Cobbler, or Freshwater Catfish, and even that isn't on the menu.

Before we leave we meet a net-maker who's come in from Broome for six weeks' work. He tells us a story of a bloke he used to fish with.

'Mad bastard,' he says. 'Got sick of his missus screwing around so he comes home one night and tells her if she's still there when he gets back he's going to shoot her.

'Goes down to his workshop, unlocks the safe and gets the gun out, comes home again to find the silly bitch asleep.'

He pauses his story to join a new roll of twine.

'So what happened?' I'm impatient.

'What do you reckon? He shot her, didn't he. Right through the back of the head. Townsfolk didn't think much of it though, so once he got out he had to move his operation up north. That's where I worked for him.

'Funny bloke to work for, though. Quiet sort of a fella. Wouldn't pick him for a murderer. Mind you, when he said jump I got up as high as I could. Man of his word and all.'

Stage One of the Ord River Scheme saw the development of roughly fifteen thousand hectares of farmland given over mainly to sugar cane, citrus, mangoes and melons. Later came the Sandalwood plantations (a peculiar crop that needs the roots of host trees or grasses in order to grow), and they've dabbled with cotton and rice among other experimental crops, but ostensibly the mix now is pretty much as it was from the start.

From the outset, the Ord Irrigation Scheme was hyped as the new MIA*. It was going to take advantage of a reliable and plentiful water source and become Australia's food bowl of the north. It was to be our great wet hope. We were all ready for it to deliver, we all believed. Stage Two was just around the corner. We could almost taste the fruit.

But nothing happened. For a very long time nothing happened.

Every now and then a new batch of believers would reignite the debate, water storage and allocations would be discussed, environmental issues would be addressed, native titles would be negotiated, the state government would start scratching around in the biscuit tin for loose change, enthusiasm would be rekindled, and a well-researched, hard-earned nothing would be the outcome yet again.

Now, with the rest of Australia drying up, the debate is on the table again. Even as I write there is a senator-led task force (they all get their own task force when they come up here: it's the modern-day equivalent of a posse) exploring northern Australia in search of water, sweet water, to take some of the load off the growers in the MIA.

Naturally they came to the Ord and, upon finding so much nothing their eyes wept real tears, they declared, 'As you were,' and left for greener pastures. Nothing, it seems, would stand in the way of the senator and his merry band of diviners finding nothing of their own.

In short and in a less cryptic spirit of communication, the state government has been seriously looking at Stage Two again, and recently called for expressions of interest from developers to open up the new irrigable land. Unfortunately the numbers didn't stack up for the developers if they were to absorb the cost of infrastructure. So they put that cost back onto the government, who in turn shit themselves and had to be excused from the discussion table.

Luckily the federal government were waiting outside and, motivated by the ongoing drought faced by the rest of the country, agreed to step in and clean up the mess. So now we have an almost water-tight (sorry) guarantee that federal money will be added to state money to ensure Stage Two goes ahead.

But so far, guess what's happened?

Less than a hundred kilometres up the road at Wyndham is a working port, primarily engaged in the export of live cattle and nickel, and the import of fuel. During the middle of the last century the local publican died one Sunday morning, and as was the custom up here in the hot climate they had him buried by sundown. Unfortunately by Monday morning they realised they'd buried him with the keys to the bar in his pocket, so they dug him up again to right the wrong. Point being, Wyndham is a town used to sorting things out quickly and, if it had to upgrade the port facilities to handle the export of Ord Irrigation produce on a major scale to Asia and beyond, they'd probably have it done before the pub shut.

The completion of the rail link between Darwin and Alice Springs also offers another national freight option, though it's probably best they don't wait for a Katherine–Kununurra link, given how long it took to finish the other one.

And there's money in the biscuit tin.

But if Stage Two doesn't go ahead the scheme is destined to remain the agricultural underachiever many believe it is. The sugar cane industry will cease due to poor economies of scale (the long-patient Koreans have already pulled out), the necessary research and development for the cotton industry to successfully infiltrate the Ord will never get done, and the Sandalwood plantations owned and run by the management investment schemes (city-based superannuation funds) will eventually take over and they might just as well erect a big white elephant for the tourists to ogle.

Of course many believe that's exactly what should happen to Kununurra.

The environmental lobby will never be convinced that irrigation is a good thing for our fragile old land, and that nothing good will ever come of clearing more land.

Native title activists will argue that the land should be left to its original custodians.

Those opposed to genetic modification will argue strongly that cotton should never be granted exemption on the grounds that it is primarily a textile crop, because cottonseed oil is a food source, and the waste product fed to cattle eventually becomes one.

Yet others will question the economic sense of the exercise even if it does succeed agriculturally. When the whole Ord River business was first tabled back in the 1950s, even Prime Minister Menzies was doubtful, saying something along the lines of, 'Yes, you can grow things up in the north, but at what price?'

Whatever your position, one thing is for certain: the world is not becoming any less populated and the food we eat has to come from somewhere.

* Murrumbidgee Irrigation Area.

OF CARAVANS AND CAMELS

The newest term for the Grey Nomads is the Silver Tsunami. I learn this at Fitzroy Crossing, in the enormous caravan park out the back of the pub. I stopped here the last time I came through –

on the 1990 trip – and there wasn't a caravan in sight. Today it's like a suburb of little mobile houses, many of them not so little. There's no doubt we're witnessing a social phenomenon here; with the onset of cheaper flights and dearer fuel, bus tours have been hit hard, and the era of the independent traveller is well and truly with us.

Once upon a time not so long ago, these outback roads were only for the truly adventurous – now the country's been opened up like a banana.

With a minimum of preparation you can tow a van across the Tanami, or the Gibb River Road, or even the Simpson Desert. There are very few stretches of dirt left in the country you can't negotiate on one tank of fuel. Nearly every remote service station has a caravan park out the back. And it's almost impossible to spend a whole day driving anywhere without seeing another traveller. Winter time on Cape York is more like Pitt Street these days than the serious driving odyssey it was two decades ago.

So where do you go to find adventure now?

Maybe the question should be how, not where, for surely the essence of travel is still about the journey and not the destination.

I meet a man in Broome who needed to clear his head, so he went for a walk. He needed to clear his head because it was, in his words, full of shit. Previously he'd been involved in a highly lucrative occupation in Melbourne – one requiring skills not necessarily taught at any of the accredited learning institutions – and for the sake of his health he headed to Broome and became a cameleer.

Logically he chose as travelling companions for his walk two camels, one large and one small. I asked him if they were good company.

'Well they don't jump up in your lap like a cat or a dog,' he told me. 'But, yeah, they're affectionate enough. When I first got the big one he used to put his head on my shoulder, you know. Just about broke my collarbone, but I guess it was his way of getting to know me.'

Together they walked over six hundred kilometres and he cites as one of the highlights the people who stopped to share a cold beer with him on the side of the road.

'One day I'd just had a couple of beers with one mob who stopped, and I was just walking along playing air guitar on my empty stubby, thinking it'd be great if some other bugger stopped with more beer, and sure enough he did, you know? A bloke and his wife pulled up with some coldies and got the deck chairs out and we sat there and had a yarn and a beer together.'

'You realise that's one of your three wishes used up, don't you?'

'Yeah, probably. And that was the same stretch of road where the two girls pulled up.'

'What two girls?'

'I never got their names. Just two beautiful girls who stopped to take a photo. And hung around, you know. Never got to my destination that night. And I'm not saying they were beautiful because I'd been out in the scrub for so long; they were lovely girls. I still think about them.'

'That's two of your wishes gone.'

He laughs, then tells me about bogging his big camel up to his belly in a mudflat, and having to dig him out before the tide came in.

'Eight hundred kilos of camel, plus a couple of hundred in the gear he was carrying, stuck fast. And he was quivering and shaking, you know, like camels do, and I had to get him out like you get a car out of a bog, with sticks and branches and blankets stuffed around his legs to give him some purchase. But I got him out, eventually.'

'Did he thank you?'

'Yeah, he did. They know when you're there for them, I reckon. Probably didn't thank me much for getting him stuck in the first place, but he was grateful when I got him out.'

He tells me he only rode for about ten or fifteen kilometres of the trip, after he'd given himself a blister wearing thongs.

'I made the mistake of overdressing.'

And I ask him if the walk changed him and he tells me he's the same man, only clearer.

'Probably still full of shit, you know, but less of it.'

Something about that statement reminds me of us in our campervans and caravans, with satellite dishes for the TV, and UHF radios, and boats and spare cars and bicycles and whatever else we can shoehorn in from home. And I wonder how we'll be travelling in another decade or two. With even more of the trappings? Or will the cost of fuel or the impact of global warming have killed off recreational travel, and forced us back to simpler modes of transport? Like camels, for instance.

The last thing my cameleer and I talk about is love, and he figures he's due after a walk like that.

'Wouldn't mind finding a nice girl and having a family, you know?'

And I could swear he's putting his third wish out there.

ANOTHER TIME

There's a lot of driving involved in getting around the northwest corner, so unless you're stopping at every chance – Bungle Bungles, Wolfe Creek, Geikie Gorge and the like – prepare for some long stretches without much variation in the scenery. Sure, there's an interesting rock formation or two, and at the right time of year the wildflowers are in bloom, but sustaining a game of I

Spy would be a struggle.

But when you reach Broome, all is forgotten. There is nowhere else in Australia like Broome. From the surreal colour of the water to the mix of old and new, it's like a town manufactured for a South Sea Island movie set.

December 1990: There is a sense one gets about places and people, a first impression that is neither visual nor auditory, nor indeed any of the five recognised senses, rather all of them combined with a little something added. I guess it amounts to instinct, and Broome grabs mine by the scruff of the neck and says, 'You're bloody welcome.'

I feel it driving in past the airport, at first glimpse of the old quarter, with the smell of the tropical vegetation thick on the breeze, in the smiles of the locals. I sense it in the slower pace of the life being lived here. I see it in the swagger of the young black kids walking down the street, and in the sway of the palm trees. I know it in my heart more than my head: Broome is the pearl, not just its mother.

I'd say most of that still holds true, though this time around I see a little more stagger than swagger in the town camps, and the laid-back pace has been cranked up a notch. Indeed, the amount of new development is astounding, especially medium-density housing, with smart, tropical-design units with water views going up everywhere.

There's no doubt Broome is flourishing, though I'm told it's been steady growth rather than a boom. It's mainly tourism driven, but there's also some pressure coming from the mining sector, with some serious offshore oil and gas exploration at Browse Basin and a few nearby terrestrial mining concerns.

With China's economy in full cry, our resource sector is stretched to the limit trying to meet the demand, and Queensland and Western

Australia in particular are doing well. Which is all good for the country: a buoyant mining industry means royalty money in the coffers, well-paid work for many and a low unemployment rate overall. In spite of the drought, the drop in Australia's GDP in the 2007 financial year was negligible thanks to the mining sector.

But there is a price to pay. The lure of the mines is contributing to the critical labour shortage in the bush, with many other enterprises relying on the backpacker and Grey Nomad labour forces to survive. And the new wealth is creating a two-paced economy out here, resulting in a higher cost of living, including a massive hike in real estate prices. In the south-east of the continent, mortgagee-in-possession sales are hitting record highs, while in the north-west you're lucky to find a house to buy, let alone afford – unless, of course, you work in the mines.

So who does work in the mines? I say goodbye to Broome and head south to find out.

ANOTHER WORLD

They're a world apart, these mining towns in Western Australia, and Newman's as 'out there' as any. It reminds me of a government housing development: functional, clean and soulless. I guess it's like mining towns anywhere, really, where almost everyone is attracted by the money. I've no doubt many mine workers genuinely enjoy their work, but it's the money that motivates most to swap their conventional lives elsewhere for a hardhat, fluoro jacket and a donga in a dustbowl.

But I don't see obvious displays of wealth around. Sure, there's the odd new 4WD about, and the roadside memorials are of a higher quality than elsewhere – I even saw one in traditional marble on the drive out – but the houses are modest-looking and largely devoid of conventional suburban trimmings such as established gardens and landscaping. There's a distinct air of impermanence to the place, even noticeable in casual conversation.

'I'll stick around as long as there's a mine here,' a born-and-bred local tells me without prompting. He used to be a butcher, but he hung up his knives and got his operator's ticket. He tells me he now earns three times as much as he did butchering. Eighty to a hundred grand a year is a base wage in most mines, and you can easily double that if you've got a coveted trade. I ask him what he spends his money on.

'Just bought myself a new car. And next year I'm going around the world.'

'No real estate?'

'Nah, not ready. Too expensive, anyway.'

A house in Newman, when they do get offered for sale, will cost over five hundred thousand. On the coast at nearby Port Hedland you won't get much under three-quarters of a million. Rental properties are almost impossible to find and very expensive when you do. Most companies provide accommodation, either in the way of houses and semi-permanent transportables for town living, or the on-site demountables (colloquially known as dongas) for the fly-in, fly-out crews.

Most of the mining sites these days have their own airstrip, so the workers need never come to town at all. Indeed, most companies don't even bother with towns anymore; they just set up their makeshift settlements at the sites and fly their staff in and out as required. It's a fragmented lifestyle for the mine workers, and some employers are now looking at returning to the more permanent town-based approach, believing it makes for a more settled and therefore happier staff.

I visit a site of one of the new kids on the block. Their story is the kind we all love to hear: the little guy takes on the big guys and beats them at their own game.* I've chosen this company because I want to interview a young woman who's swapped a life in the rag trade in Sydney to come and work for them. With young people coming from all over for a piece of the action, I figured her story was about as radical as any to highlight the trend.

She turns out a sweetheart. Not only is she a sort – even in 'hi-vis' fluoro mine clobber – but she's good radio talent, and she's got a laugh that stops you in your tracks.

She's twenty-eight years old, and when she first told her Paddington friends she was giving up the café culture to go bush and work in the mines they thought she was mad. Now they quiz her about how much money she earns and ask questions like, 'Do you think I could handle it out there too?'

And she reckons the biggest trap with the big money is to 'live a fabulous life and end up with nothing to show for your time in the mines but a few overseas holidays and a new car'.

So I ask her what she's been doing with her money.

'Just that,' she says. 'Holidays, new cars.' Then she laughs that disarming laugh of hers, and tells me the company encourages its staff to have a five-year plan to avoid becoming trapped in the money cycle. Her plan includes setting up her own fashion business so she's got something to go on with and, of course, a few more holidays in the meantime. She's blond and svelte and it's easy to imagine her making the switch back to the rag trade, but there's something even more interesting about a beautiful woman in a hardhat and blue jeans.

'What beats you in the end?' I ask. 'The heat? The dust? The isolation?'

'Different for everyone, I think. For me it'll probably be missing the finer things a girl likes to have.'

'Can't be any shortage of suitors out here.'

'No, there are many men. And you know they're all on good

money, too. It's like the ultimate hunting ground, really.'

Then she laughs again and I'm sorry it's all over. And for just a moment I let myself dream of giving in to a woman like that; but then again, which one would I love? The city girl with the unusual job? Or the shapely blond with the tumble-down laugh living in the donga next door? I wake up to myself and *The Parrot* and I move on. Life's complicated enough as it is.

* At the time of publication the 'new kids on the block' were still powering ahead, getting their first shipment of ore off to China pretty much on schedule in spite of significant hurdles. Which I guess now makes the little guy a big guy, and no longer entitled to the underdog status I've given him.

PLAIN DRIVING

I feel like a human iron, the land's so flat. Not a crease, not a stain, nothing but an endless grey line across a monotonous paisley shirt, the pattern for which is determined by the wildflowers in purple, pink and maroon. And I know that sounds spectacular, but I swear they blend in with the landscape, as if they've come from the red soil and daren't stray too far before they return to it. And they don't tend to mix, so you get great fields of one muted colour, followed by great fields of another, occasionally separated by one solitary yellow bush.

Indeed, they're so much a part of the landscape's natural palette that I once even stopped to take a photo of a striking red bush only to discover it was a non-flowering bush covered in red dust. The soil was more vibrant than the flowers.

After Newman I pull off the road every twenty kilometres or so to allow the passing of a demountable house bound for the mines, or sometimes a piece of mining equipment so wide I'm forced to go bush to avoid it.

If you ever doubted the health of the resource sector, this drive alone would be enough to convince you.

The weather changes on the way south, and by the time I reach Mount Magnet a chill wind has picked up, apparently not for the first time here. On the way into town I notice a sign promoting Cold Beer at one of the pubs, and some wit had scrubbed out the 'B'.

At the service station I get talking to a couple of bikers from one of the country's more notorious motorcycle gangs. They're headed for the coast after a long trip across country.

'To get out of the bloody desert,' one of them tells me. 'Sick of seeing the same thing all day.'

Hear, hear. I ask him how big the gang is and he tells me they don't divulge that sort of information.

At that point I figure an interview is probably out of the question.

His mate is an altogether different proposition, and once he works out he recognises me from the television he wants to chat. It's an interesting contrast: a big, hard-looking, heavily tattooed man kitted out in full bikie colours wanting to make friends. I feel like I'm being licked by a lion.

On the drive east towards Leinster I see more Wedge-tailed Eagles than I've seen in my life in total. Along with the crows and kites, they thrive on the road kill left in the wake of the most common country tragedy. For a while it was thought Wedgie numbers Australia-wide were in serious decline. The belief was that agricultural chemicals were infiltrating their food chain and causing the birds to lay thin-shelled eggs, which broke before they hatched. But I'm pleased to report they're doing just fine, at least out here in south-central Western Australia: quite possibly an indirect result of increased traffic on these roads, thanks to the mining boom.

When I reach the mining town of Leinster I'm not surprised to see it signposted as The Home of the Wedge-tailed Eagle. I casually suggest at the service station that the community should erect a bronze statue of the eagle, but I'm told nothing happens in town without the mining company's approval.

'It's a closed community,' I'm told. 'So unless you work for the company you can't stay, and even if you do you can't do much else. And anyway, I doubt they'd care about a bird, even if they did help save it.'

The large print giveth and the small print taketh away.

From Leinster I pass through Leonora and Menzies and maybe one or two other towns I've forgotten. Basically it's more of the same, and I reach Kalgoorlie just after dark.

That night I dream of plains, great plains of nothing, and not much else besides.

NEW TRICKS

Kalgoorlie was built on gold and girls: when the mines boomed, the brothels flourished. On the strength of this I assumed Hay Street would be raging, surrounded by a mining industry in full cry. Not so.

With fly-in, fly-out rosters and mining companies encouraging the men to bring their families with them, even the oldest profession is struggling to survive.

So what's a working girl to do but diversify into tourism? Now the three main brothels operating on what's left of The Golden Mile all offer 'working brothel' tours. At given intervals through the afternoon, giggling gaggles of tourists are shown through the premises to marvel at what was – and still is – on offer.

According to the caretaker of the one I visit – she is managing operations while the madam is away – these days they make more from tourism than they do from selling sex.

'So what kind of woman works in a brothel?'

'We get quite a few married women,' the caretaker tells me. 'Sometimes their husbands don't know. But sometimes the husbands even drop them off to work, which I find hard to fathom.

'The rest are younger girls, often university students from interstate who travel west to work for a week or two before returning to school, cashed up and ready for a new semester.

'But it's not an industry to take on long term. It takes its toll on the girls, physically and mentally. We try to encourage them to have a five-year plan, then get out.'

I note the similarity with the mines, and, just like the miners, she tells me not many sex industry workers walk away with enough to start afresh either.

'The saddest case I remember was a woman with four kids whose ex-husband wasn't paying any maintenance. So she had the flash car, the big house, but couldn't afford the private school fees for her kids. And for the entire time she worked for us she watched that front door, living in dread that someone she knew would walk through.'

'What do the girls do when that happens?'

'They run out the back door!'

I meet one of the girls: a handsome woman with a diamond stud in one of her upper canines, wearing a towel on her freshly washed hair. She is all charm and confidence, but something about her bravado is unconvincing. I ask her what triggered the switch from amateur to professional and she tells me she was happily married and one day she walked in on her husband in bed with a hooker.

'So I thought, "If it's a hooker you want, then that's what I'll be. Only I'll do it better." Now I travel the world, have a great life, and get paid for what I used to give away for free.'

She's all clichés, and ready to shock at any opportunity. I ask her how the partnered girls reconcile what they do for a living with their private lives.

'Personally, I couldn't do it,' she says. 'How can you tell someone you love them, then come to work and suck other men's cocks?'

I was trying to interview her for the radio and every time she started talking about something interesting she'd throw it away with a crudity designed to jolt my senses. It was all part of the ritual she'd developed to keep herself afloat, to maintain the stereotype. If I'd had more time I might have been able to get something real from her, but she was a busy girl. She had a date with the hairdresser, then an appointment with a regular.

'He likes it rough, you know,' she tells me. 'But they all want cuddles in the end.'

She does have time to tell me she's something of a celebrity, having recently featured in a magazine spread. Then she reveals a part of herself that no amount of cosmetic surgery can remove.

'The number of guys who came up to me on the street after that article and said, "Thank you so much, you really touched me with what you said." I couldn't believe it.'

Her empathy was with the guys, not the girls.

She also tells me almost everyone working in brothels has been abused in some way as a child. I suspect what she's really saying is that's her story, but I daresay it's not an uncommon one.

I ask her how long she thinks she can continue in this line of work.

'Oh, I don't know, darling. Everyone here's looking for a sugar daddy to rescue them.'

Then she stands and adjusts the towel she's wearing on her head to signal my time is up.

'I'm just staying clear of the drugs and building my financial security,' she pauses a beat, then concludes the sentence by reminding me what it is they do around here. And with a smile she turns and leaves.

Meanwhile a new tour group has gathered in the foyer and she tosses off a wisecrack as she passes. The group laughs, and I imagine she'd make the perfect tour guide: the 'brassy hooker with a heart of gold' for an audience expecting nothing less.

LATE BLOOMING

Okay, I take it all back: the wildflowers in the south-west are lovely.

To begin with, the soil isn't as red as it is in the north, so the purples and pinks of the flowers tend to stand out more, as do the olive green and copper brown trunks of the mallee trees, and the impossibly pink Salmon Gums. Throw in a blue sky and a blotch of red grevillea here and there and it all starts to look like the landscape was painted by a three-year-old child.

Then with altitude comes the glades of black boys, with their glossy sheen and mop tops, the stringybarks, mountain gums and banksias, and lining the roadside all the way are independent splashes of colour: blue leschenaultias, yellow buttercups and wattles, orange hibbertias, white daisies, purple hoveas, orchids of every imaginable colour, not forgetting the green and vivid red of the Kangaroo Paws.

Not a bad show, I guess, but right now I'm more concerned with *The Parrot*. We've shared the odd misadventure of late and she looks a bit sad and sorry. And I'm not talking about the scratches and dents I've picked up along the way – normal wear and tear I'm calling that stuff – but the latest damage to the back end of her. It looks like her arse has dropped.

It all started back when I knocked the tailpipe off going through that ditch in the Territory. I had it reattached but I must have jarred the rear plastic bumper in the process because half of it fell off, taking the number plate with it. The other half is still hanging on, but it's not an attractive sight.

So I've had a new half sent to Perth, from Germany, and hopefully a new set of plates. While I wait for my parts I'm hanging out in Lancelin, just to the north of Perth.

Lancelin's a seaside resort town famous for crayfish and windsurfing. Right now though it feels more like an Antarctic base station with the filthy weather going on around me; I'm tempted to get a slab of beer and wait it out like we used to do with cyclones in the Territory. Instead I bunker down to read the local paper and find this in the wanted section:

> **Singing teacher** with a sense of humour to teach a group of non-singers. Teachers and 'singers' contact ...

That sounds like a lark, so I ring. Initially she's distrustful and I have a hard time convincing her I'm not out to make them all look like fools. She tells me she's had a few nuisance calls, along with a job offer – yes, a bona fide job offer – so now she vets the calls thoroughly because it seems the world is full of nutters. Somehow I convince her I'm not (I have experience in this) and she agrees to meet me.

She's a physio in town and one of her elderly clients was bemoaning the fact that she wasn't game to get up and sing when it was called for – weddings, funerals, anything – because her friends had convinced her she sounded like a choking animal. So they decided to get all the non-singers together and find a teacher with humour enough to laugh with them, but not at them, for singing lessons.

Sensibly, alcohol was to play an important part in preparations, and anyone who turned up for lessons who could actually sing was to be shown the door immediately.

'My low point came when I was vacuuming the house with headphones on,' she tells me, 'singing away at the top of my voice.

'And I turned around to see my two teenage children doubled up in fits of laughter at the noise I was making.

'So I thought, "That's it: I'm going to learn to sing."

'So now we've got ourselves a teacher and we're having our first lesson next week.'

'What was the job offer?' I ask.

'They wanted us to sing carols at the Christmas pageant. But I don't think even Christ is ready to forgive that crime.

'It's an ongoing thing,' she continues. 'I think people in this country are retiring when they should be re-firing. Change jobs, keep going, keep learning, stay active, mentally as well as physically.

'A friend of mine was recently telling me about his mother, who's ninety-two, lives at home, no aids, and she's just joined the gym. Ninety-two years old and she's off to the gym three times a week. Now how's that for late blooming?'

How's that indeed: ninety-two and still game to wear lycra tights. And why not? She couldn't look any worse than *The Parrot*.

CAUGHT HAPPY

While I'm waiting for *The Parrot* to be serviced I spend the day in Perth, just wandering around the malls, talking to people and drinking coffee. At one stage I buy *The Big Issue* magazine. I like this concept: giving those people doing it a bit tough a legitimate way to earn a quid – each street vendor gets half the proceeds of every magazine sold – and there's usually at least one quality article in every issue, which is more than I can say for most of the mainstream glossies.

In this issue it's a piece on happiness, and the cover carries one of the most endearing photos of a happy face I've ever seen. It's of a man of about forty, with a stubbled crown atop a clean-shaven round face, slits for eyes, and a closed-mouth smile that stretches from one cheek to the other. He looks like the wide-mouthed frog with a belly full of flies.

In the editorial he says what makes him happy is 'when the sun is shining and everyone is smiling'. And he says the happiest he's been was when he got married, and his mum made it down from the country for his big day.

And as I sit on the Murray Street cobblestones in the sunshine, reading the article and listening to a half-decent busker work through his repertoire, I decide the wide-mouthed frog had it about right. Occasionally passers-by look quizzically at me sitting on the ground, but as soon as I smile and wave they drop their guards and respond in kind, instinctively and unstintingly.

Caught happy, if only for a moment, by a smile from a stranger sitting in the sunshine.

But nothing lasts forever and by the time the van is ready the sun has been blotted out by rainclouds. I drive south to Mandurah in the rain and book into a caravan park. The manager recognises me from the television and I tell her I'm sourcing radio stories, so she says she'll have a think about the possibilities in the area.

Half an hour later she knocks on the Hymer's door.

'How does a direct descendant of Davy Crockett's sound?' she says. 'Is that quirky enough for you?'

'Absolutely.'

'Oh, and I just happened to mention to one of my friends, who's a single woman of about sixty-five, that you were staying in the park. And that you were on your own.'

'And?'

'And she wants to know if it's experience you're looking for.'

And here I was thinking I'd lost my touch.

AMERICAN LEGENDS

Davy Crockett was the quintessential hero of the American Wild West. Born in the late 1700s in Tennessee, by his own account he had already killed a bear before he was three years old, and that was only the beginning. By the time he was killed at the Battle of the Alamo in 1836, outnumbered and overpowered by the troops of the equally colourful Mexican president-turned-dictator Antonio Lopez de Santa Anna, his portfolio included: trapper, pioneer, adventurer, philanthropist, soldier, state assemblyman and congressman. He was not yet fifty years old.

His legend has been glorified in film, print, song and television. At the height of the craze in the mid-1950s, American children could choose from over three thousand Davy Crockett toys and it was estimated that 10 per cent of all children's clothes were linked to the craze. The coonskin caps in particular were highly prized.

His favourite rifle, 'Old Betsy', is still on display at The Alamo Chapel in Texas.

But, according to his descendants now living larger than life in

Mandurah, Western Australia, David Crockett, as he was known in his lifetime, was nothing more than a wild boy who loved trouble.

'Oh a lot of it was myth, I'm afraid,' Mrs Crockett, the matriarch of the family, says with a distinct American accent. 'He was just a wild, footloose old boy, you know, and wherever there was a fight or a bunch of Indians he would just rush there. He was interested in action.'

'Action man,' adds one of her daughters, while the other daughter agrees with some volubility.

I'm interviewing the two daughters along with their mother because they were sitting at either end of the table, like bookends, and there was no way I could have kept them out of it. None of these women are shy, by any stretch, but the daughters crank loud up a notch.

The connection with the legend is with Mrs Crockett's late husband, who was Davy Crockett's great-great-great-nephew. Not a strong connection, I'll grant you, but if personality traits are anything to go by, it does seem as though the Crockett gene for action is manifest here at the dining table before me.

This line of the family was from Montana, and they emigrated to Australia about forty years ago, when the kids were still teenagers. Apparently the old boy had a bit of the Crockett adventurer in him as well, and he decided it would be a good idea to buy a couple of cattle stations in the West Kimberley.

'He thought Australia sounded like a good place for a rancher to be. So he gave me a choice between some horrible place in Alaska …'

'Where there were lots of tall, black bears', interrupts one of the daughters.

'Kodiak bears!' says the other daughter.

'So you figured kangaroos would be a better bet,' I squeeze in.

'Oh, much better,' says Mrs Crockett. 'But not in the water

tank.'

'That was about the first time the charm wore thin,' remembers one daughter, 'when we found a couple of dead kangaroos in the rainwater tank.'

How they got there is anyone's guess, but Mrs Crockett moved herself into town pretty soon thereafter and swore she never drank tank water again.

'But we loved it on the station. Mother mightn't have, but we had the best time, hunting *bungarra* (goanna) with the Aboriginal kids and helping Daddy with the mustering.'

'Remember when we got rained in that time, and you played strip poker with all the ringers and ended up with all their belts and boots and money?'

And I can see this picture as the girls recall it: half a dozen stockmen sitting around in a bush camp politely letting the brash young boss's daughter win at cards, more out of fear of her than their employer.

'Yeah, it was a bugger of a life. And remember when we were castrating the calves and you were cooking the mountain oysters on the fire, and when you bit into the first one thirty ringers sitting on the fence crossed their legs?'

And so flow the reminiscences, each delivered at speed and volume, often corrected by their mother.

One of the daughters had worked in Aboriginal health in the Kimberley, and talks about the leprosy problem still rife in Aboriginal communities as late as the mid-1970s, before sulphur treatments brought it under control.

She remembers sending message sticks into the Warburton Ranges community – normally closed to non-Aboriginal people – in order to gain approval to conduct morbidity checks, and once inside finding the same problems inherent in communities today. She tells me one of their preferred substances before alcohol was prepared from the bark of a particular tree, which they charred to ash and mixed with their chewing tobacco. They called it *nikki nikki* and the effect was like that of any other central nervous system depressant, such as grog. So even without white-man's alcohol they were finding ways to get wasted.

We talk of the 'Bradshaw' art in the area, and the 'spaceman' paintings found on the caves on their properties (the like of which feature in von Daniken's controversial *Chariots of the Gods* book), and of crocodiles, and of cultural differences between Americans and Australians, and many things besides.

And in the midst of all the stories and rebuttals and contradictions and general chaos and din, is laughter, much laughter.

Towards the end of my visit I ask Mrs Crockett how old her man was when he died, and when she tells me I make the mistake of suggesting eighty-five was a good innings.

'Yes, until you get there,' she says. 'And then it's not nearly enough. Then you want a hundred.'

'I'm shootin' for a hundred.' Guess who.

'Me too. There's no way I'll be ready to go at eighty-five.' The other bookend.

And I'm backing them in. After all, these people are Crocketts, and Crocketts don't go down without a fight. Remember the Alamo?

You may all go to hell, and I will go to Texas.

State assemblyman David Crockett, on the eve of his defection from Tennessee politics to Texas.

NO YELLOW DOGS

I've just travelled from Mandurah, Western Australia, to Ceduna, South Australia, and not found a story to excite me.

When I was driving through outback Queensland I came across a yellow dog hung from a signpost. A big male dingo, scalped for bounty and hanging by one leg; obviously put there for a reason by someone who thought it worth their time and effort to make whatever point they were trying to make. Now that, to me, had all the hallmarks of a good story.*

Now here I am on the other side of the Nullarbor empty-handed, like the nothingness of the place robbed me of any chance I had of finding anything. I had several half-leads along the way, a few starts that stopped prematurely, but nothing amounting to a story.

I did have one notable conversation with a hitchhiker I picked up and took through to Esperance. He was a twenty-year-old German from Koln, who'd been in the country for nine months. He'd just finished a short stint of planting Blue Gum seedlings in Albany for $16.50 an hour. I asked what concerned him.

'Racism,' he said, without hesitation. 'Back home in Germany I had this impressions of Jewish peoples that they are all bad. Since I am travelling I have met some Jewish peoples who are good people, just like you and me, and I have changed my thinking on this.'

'Have you seen racism in Australia?' I asked him.

'Oh, yes. There is much racism against the Aborigine peoples. I believe it is everywhere in the world. It is natural to like some people and not like others so much, but we should not be deciding this according to what country they are coming from, or what colour they are, I think.'

Yet another remorseful German wandering the globe doing good work.

My latest story attempt is to cover the 'Nullarbor Golf Course' yarn: a few enterprising souls have hatched a plan to build the world's longest course, stretching from Kalgoorlie to Ceduna – or vice versa if you're travelling the other way – with a hole at each of the roadstops along the way, for an overall distance of about fourteen hundred kilometres.

But after about four stops and some quality grabs from each of the groundsmen-elect about golfers falling in wombat holes and crows thieving golf balls, the microphone and I have a disagreement and I lose everything.

So I start again but I draw a blank with the next couple of stops and it's starting to look like I'm going to bed without any supper – it's always hard re-recording a story when you've lost the juice – and I'm feeling very much out of sync with the universe.

And I'm standing in the middle of the plain with no trees, absently pissing on the dirt and wondering how dogs get on out here, yellow or otherwise, when a gust of wind hits me and turns the arc I'm making back on itself, and therefore myself. And it's all so apt I don't even curse.

Of course one symptom of this condition is the propensity to make bad judgement calls, and I missed two stories on the way across the Nullarbor as a consequence.

The first was a Japanese cyclist about a third of the way across the plain. Now, human endeavour doesn't get a whole lot crazier than this. It's hot, it's flat, and the stretches between roadstops can top two hundred kilometres. I've heard some of these kamikaze adventurers sleep on the side of the road with the snakes and the scorpions, and Christ only knows what they make of wombats, camels and emus when they wet themselves at the sight of a koala.

So I stopped. Both he and his bike were lying on their sides in the gravel, and when I pulled up beside him he smiled but made no move to get up. It looked like he'd just pushed himself as far as he could go, then said 'Bugger it!' (or whatever the equivalent is in Japanese) and just stopped pedalling and let everything fall-down-dead. He was a nice-looking kid, maybe twenty-five years old, with a heavy tan so he'd probably been on the road a week or two and had a few stories to tell. So I exchanged a few words with him, determined his English wasn't fluent enough to carry an interview, wished him luck, and drove off.

In retrospect I'm sure his accent would have only enhanced the interview, giving the 'stranger in a strange land' element a boost, but I completely missed that at the time and drove away from what could have been a great little story.

The second was the eccentric American vigneron who's trialling ten acres of Cabernet Sauvignon on the edge of the Nullarbor. Apparently some vineyard consultant guru assessed the Nullarbor and found the soil types to be almost identical to those in the Napa Valley in California, and declared there was no reason vineyards couldn't be grown for the entire length of the plain. So our mad Yank bought up some coastal land for a song, put in a desalination plant to convert the seawater and bores to tap into the subterranean reserves, and presto, he's a Nullarbor winemaker.

I'm told he thinks Australians are basically morons who haven't got a clue how to utilise what they've got in their own country. And, who knows, he might be right, and in ten years we'll all be congratulating him for showing us the way. In the meantime – whether he's right or wrong – I'd be happy to have just one character a week like that to interview for the show.

So there were two yellow dogs hanging by the roadside in plain sight, and I drove right on by.

Add to this pathetic summary the fact that the new bumper I had fitted it Perth has melted and fallen off somewhere along the Nullarbor. It seems it wasn't my ditch-jumping that caused the first one to rattle loose, but the angle of the newly reattached tailpipe, which is now blowing hot exhaust onto the plastic bumpers and melting them and blackening the arse end of the rig in the process. Oh dear. The owners will be thinking I'm out here trying to kill the poor old *Parrot* off.

* Naturally I didn't follow the original yellow dog lead either, but I did stop to take his photo.

BOMBED, BLOWN AND BURNT

Back in the late 1950s, when the British were setting off nuclear bombs at Maralinga, nobody had a clue they were creating a tourist attraction-in-waiting. We know this because we had a hell of a time getting them to pay for any of the clean-up, and if they had any inkling that there'd be money in it further down the track they'd have given us nothing.*

But fast forward almost fifty years and that's exactly what we've got: a nuclear tourist attraction, complete with an authenticated history, actual disused buildings where the three thousand or so scientists and military personnel lived, worked and played while blowing up the surrounding countryside, and presumably even real atomic bomb sites!

While it's not my idea of a holiday destination, apparently it's a growing niche market worldwide, and in Ceduna I meet a man who's in the final stages of developing the concept for the traditional owners, the Maralinga Tjarutja people.

'It was a long process,' he says, ' but eventually we came up with a proposal everybody was happy with; which is basically a land-management and heritage resource centre operating primarily as a tourist attraction related to the atomic testing, managed by rangers and run the same way as you'd run a conservation park.'

'And is it safe?'

'The site's been decontaminated to World Safe Practice standards, so it now has less radioactivity than the fire alarm in your house.'

Great; I didn't know about fire alarms. I consider backtracking to see for myself, but it's too far and there's no guarantee I'll be granted access anyway, so I push on.

From Ceduna I head south down the west coast of the Eyre Peninsula, in weather wild enough to drive you to ground. Along the way I stop to talk to a roadside breadmaker. He'd been a baker by trade and decided to go back to basics and build his own oven and bake from home. Now he only bakes as many loaves as he can be bothered throwing into his Scotch Oven** (one hundred maximum), and relies on passing motorists to stop and buy from his unmanned stall.

'People will always be honest if you give them a chance to be,' he says.

He's converted an old schoolhouse for him and his family to live in, and his wife is a nurse in town. He bakes his bread, then busies himself building additions to the house for the rest of the day while he waits for his wife to finish work, and the kids to get home from school.

He notices the damage I've done to *The Parrot*.

'Yeah, I'm usually the last owner a car ever has, too,' he says.

I see his belted-up old thing in the driveway and recognise the look.

'I know what you mean, mate,' I say.

We bid farewell, brothers-in-arms.

I camp at Coffin Bay thinking the wind might drop enough by morning to catch one of the King George Whiting the area is famous for. Instead it picks up. I move on without wetting a line.

By the time I'm through Port Lincoln and driving up the east coast the gusts of wind are threatening to knock *The Parrot* off the road. I'm hoping to get to Port Augusta before dark.

Then just on the other side of Cowell I see a ferry sign. I didn't even know there was a ferry service here. I take the road and end up in Lucky Bay, a quaint little holiday town consisting of a hundred odd shacks – and for some this is a kind exaggeration – all clinging to a narrow strip along the beach.

I'm in luck and a ferry to the Yorke Peninsula leaves in a couple of hours.

I amuse myself reading a local paper and discover there's been a scandal in town. A visiting professional fisherman has been netting the beach in front of the shacks where the owners like to catch a fish or two, and someone has taken exception and decided to burn his car, inscribing the words 'Stop netting Lucky' in the tray of the ute before setting it alight.

Only problem with the plan was the arsonist got the wrong car.

I speak to one of the resident professional fishermen and naturally he's quick to distance himself from the interloper.

'Yeah, he causes trouble wherever he goes, that bloke,' he tells me. 'But if they've got a vendetta against fishermen, who's to say I'm safe?'

'We figure it's someone who doesn't know his car that well, maybe someone from out of town who's been paid to do the job.'

'Paid by whom?'

'Paid by someone pissed off enough to take action. Could be anyone of about fifteen people I can think of.'

'Well that narrows it down some. How many of them were here at the time?'

'Oh here we go,' he says, when he realises what I'm up to. We both laugh.

He's a jolly soul with a weather-worn face and a well-tended beer belly. As we talk he stands, leaning on the table, while I sit. He's smoking rollies in a cigarette holder, a habit he reckons he'll have to give up soon.

His wife rolls her eyes when she hears this. She's sitting on a table off to the side and listening to us talk. She helps her husband with the nets and looks like she does her fair share of the hard yards. She's a healthy-looking woman with a kind face. She's the one who keeps them living at the coast and not in their town house.

'Just gotta keep the missus off the drink is the main thing,' he says, mischievously.

'Not likely,' she says with a smile.

'Nah, she hardly drinks. Couldn't work the nets without her these days.'

They exchange a glance to ensure the balance is right.

'But if the fishing gets any worse I'll have to quit the smokes, that's for sure,' he says. 'They knock a man up too much, anyway. Either that or the sand's getting softer.'

'You better keep yourself fit, mate,' I say. 'So you can carry the water to put those fires out.'

'Nah, I've got three cars, so I could probably spare one. After that I might have to give up though.'

I leave the jolly fisherman and his wife and catch my ferry. We cross into a blood orange sunset and land at Wallaroo after dark.

*Recent UK media reports claim that the British Ministry of Defence has finally admitted responsibility for exposing service personnel to dangerous levels of radiation during the testing. Hearings are set to begin in 2009 to determine the viability of legal action for surviving test participants. For many, civilians included, it is already too late.

** While Scotch Oven appears to be a bastardised term, it is the correct one. They have their origins in the old Scottish wood/coal/peat-fired bakery ovens, but somewhere along the way they became Scotch rather than Scottish Ovens. Perhaps it was a nod to the spirit that warms every good Scottish baker in the wee small hours.

SHE MAKES IT EASY

It's a strange thing to drive through a city whose football team has just been thrashed in the grand final. At 5 pm on any other Saturday afternoon you'd be hard-pressed driving through the same city without running over a reveller spilling out of one of the pubs, but on this day the streets are empty. The pubs are full: I catch fleeting vignettes of people standing mute with drink in hand, too shocked for words yet, and not ready to leave because they have nowhere to take this feeling; they hadn't planned for it, and it's too big to deal with alone. So the streets are empty like Sunday morning.

I know the feeling but I don't care today. I used to care about sport, but something happened to me: I saw the light, went mad, whatever you think is a fair thing. All I know is I can take it or leave it these days, even if it involves my team. I know I'll never get an Order of Australia for saying this, but it is only a game, and there are more important things.

Such as picking up daughters from airports. She's the last off the plane, as usual, and smiles at me from the bottom of the walkway, as usual. Then she runs the last ten metres and jumps into my arms: my favourite usual.

And she's still young enough to gush out everything in the first two minutes: she's got my Father's Day present in her bag do I want to open it now? and she's brought her clarinet but we'll have to get a book because her best friend from school is learning too and oh, don't forget I have to ring Mum, and can we see a salt lake? and go horse riding somewhere?

And I'm sure every parent knows the comfort of that tumble of breathless nonsense.

We collect her luggage and set off through the barren streets of Adelaide, heading north.

A salt lake shouldn't prove hard to find in the state that could almost have one as its emblem, so I ask her if there's anything else on her wish list.

'How far is Ayres Rock?'

'You want to see Uluru?'

'Yeah. And a camel. I've never seen a camel up close.'

'Okay. We can do that. But there'll be some driving, to get up and back in a week.'

But she's a good traveller, is Benino. Maybe it's genetic, maybe it just is, but she rarely grumbles, she enjoys the subtle changes in vegetation and topography – which helps the long stretches – and, of course, there's always her travelling hobby to keep her occupied.

'This must be a good area along here,' she tells me.

'For what?'

'Animals. Look. There's a pile of bones every hundred metres or so.'

'That would make it a bad area for animals, then.'

'Oh, yeah.'

Straight back onto the road kill. She could easily end up a taxidermist, this kid. Or a mortician.

That night two strange things happen.

First, no sooner have we made camp and settled than my dear old mother rings. That may not seem unusual to you but my mother and I don't share what you would call a stereotypical mother and son relationship. We speak only occasionally; when we do speak it's usually fine – we just don't feel the need to do it all that often.

Anyway, uncannily she rings on the first night I've got my daughter to ask how things are going, and if I took any photos of Benino for her when I was in Cairns. (That was the last call: three months ago.)

So we have one of those absurd conversations that go around

Above: *Author and daughter, atop Uluru, Northern Territory – story page 149.*

Below: The Parrot *at large, Red Lily Lagoon, Northern Territory – story page 101.*

Above: *Stick your job, mining country, Western Australia – story page 120.*

Below: *Make your mark, mining country, South Australia.*

Above: *Roadside beauty, country and western New South Wales – story page 200.*

Below: *Don't ask me, Eyre Peninsula, South Australia – story page 139.*

Above: *Flood landscaping, northern New South Wales – story page 203.*

Below: *Flood parking, northern New South Wales – story page 203.*

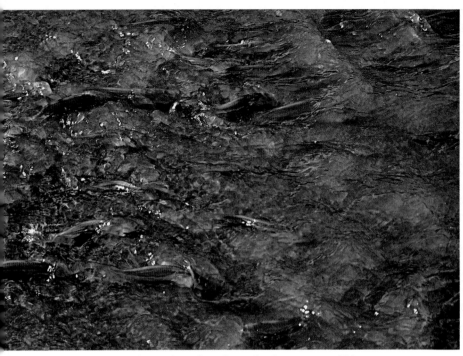

Above: *Fish crossing the road, southern Queensland – story page 226.*

Below: *Fish not crossing the road, southern Queensland – story page 226.*

Above: *One of the birds I picked up, Dorrigo, New South Wales.*

Below: *Another one: Benino in full flight, salt lake, South Australia – story page 146.*

Above: *The foxacene and the foxy– story page 240.*

Below: *Inquisitve echidna, Monaro Country, New South Wales.*

in circles and remind me of a Monty Python sketch, with Mum insisting she hasn't seen a photo of her granddaughter since she was born (not impossible, in my family, but highly improbable) and me claiming I've sent her millions of photos and please stop exaggerating or I'll die of indignation.

And the second strange thing that happens is out of the blue a friend emails a photo of me, taken twenty years ago at Yulara (the Uluru township), where we are now heading.

Sometimes it's hard not to entertain the notion that women have periscopes.

So I look at the young man in the photo with his face so fresh and trusting that he barely looks like me – indeed my friend isn't at all convinced it is me: I was completely bald then, thanks to a bout of alopecia – and I remember the fool fondly. 'A likeable rogue' was how he'd been described, and I remember enjoying the description. Now I could see there was no real rogue there, but a naïf who thought the world would always turn for him.

And I look at my sleeping Benino, a child so much like her father she could be me going around again (to try to get it right this time), and I'm thankful to have so much, for she makes it easy for me to forgive my mistakes.

SPIRITUAL CENTRES

There is a woman in Alice Springs who cooks and eats pussy cats. Indeed she cooks them so well she's even won a competition with one of her recipes.

'As part of the Festival this year there was a Wild Bush Food competition,' she tells me, 'and I just happened to have a couple of cats in the freezer, and some quandong in the larder – that's like a native peach – some native lemon grass, and that's basically it:

the Quandong Caterole.'

I was intrigued by the casual mention of cats in the freezer, so I ask if she's copped any flak from the cat-lovers.

'Yeah, there've been many, many, very nasty emails,' she says. 'Quite abominable, really. Just people who can't see beyond the emotion of their own cat, and into the lives of all the native birds and animals the feral cats are eating.'

'How did cat end up on your menu in the first place?'

'Well I knew the Aboriginal mob love pussy cat, been eating them for a hundred years or more. And our dogs used to tree the cats on our property here, and we'd dispatch them. So one day I opened one up to see what he'd been eating and found the flesh to be quite sweet.

'It was about ten years ago, the first time. I had to take a dish to a dinner party for some friends, and I just happened to have a couple of cats in the freezer at that time as well, so I cooked a caterole. Didn't tell them what was in it, and by the end of the night it was all gone. Then I told them what it was.'

'How did they respond?'

'They wanted to know if there was any more.'

Benino and I reach Uluru late in the afternoon and I can tell she's excited. So am I. I haven't climbed The Rock for twenty years and I'm looking forward to taking her up the next morning.

Since that time the ownership debate has come and gone, and the land containing Uluru and Kata Tjuta (The Olgas) is now back in the hands of the original custodians, the Anangu people. And the national park is run by a board of management that includes representatives from various Anangu and non-Anangu groups.

The Anangu would prefer we didn't climb Uluru, since it's a site of great significance to them. However, I believe Uluru is for everyone to share.

We whitefellas may not have forty thousand years' worth of

stories to support our claim, but I certainly feel drawn towards it as some sort of spiritual centre of our country, and I'm sure I'm not alone. Hordes of tourists make the climb every year, and not everyone does so simply to tick off another 'been there, done that' conquest.

Some do it to bring on a fatal heart attack, for instance, and halfway up the steep section I thought I was going to join that elite group. Benino, meanwhile, was springing up the side like a mountain goat, which I'm sure is how I approached it last time.

But, on this occasion, old man time held one hand and Benino came back to hold the other, and together we walked to the top of Uluru. And while I'm grateful I could share the experience with my daughter, I think next time around I'll be taking the advice of the traditional owners and staying on the ground.

From Uluru we're driving to Oodnadatta, and en route we stop to talk to one of the cyclists touring the country solo. This one's a raggedy-looking soul from Melbourne, who's spent the last six months riding a big loop along all the dirt roads through the centre – Strzelecki, Plenty, Tanami, Gibb River – and he's happy to be heading home.

'I've lost a lot of weight,' he tells me. 'You can only carry so much food and water on the long hauls. And, even supplementing with fresh road kill when I could, I'm down to muscle and bone.'

'What road kill?'

'Kangaroos. Rabbits. Anything fresh-killed.'

'I've recently heard pussy cats make good eating. Seen any of those?'

'Yeah, but they've all been too alive for me to catch.'

I ask him if there's been anything he's missed while he's been away.

'Nothing, really. I ring my mother up about once a week, so it'll be nice to see her. But nothing else. I've always been a bit different from other people.'

'How?'

'My values. I think too many people trap themselves with their possessions, and can't escape them to do what they want to do.'

We share a pot of tea and he eats half a packet of biscuits, so I leave him with the rest of the packet and some fruit besides. He's already eating them as we drive away.

The next pilgrimage we encounter is a small group of people stopped on the side of the Oodnadatta track, changing a tyre on one of their cars. They're on a whistle-stop tour of inland South Australia and the Northern Territory looking for spiritual connections to their land. Their leader is a reverend from a small church in Adelaide, and Uluru is their ultimate destination.

The reverend is an articulate man and I ask him if what he's looking for is similar to the things Bruce Chatwin wrote about in *The Songlines*, a book hypothesising how Aboriginal people make connections with their land by mapping it out in story and song.

'That's what this particular trip is all about,' he tells me. 'I have, over the past ten years or so, had conversations with Aboriginal elders about their dreaming stories, and pieced together my own map of this area so we white people might be able do our own "sorry business" for what we're doing to the land.

'I've had Aboriginal elders say to me, "Look, you can't dance our corroborees – even if you learn the moves you have no connection with the dances so there'll be no power – so go away and learn your own dances and come and dance with us, because the land desperately needs it."

'And I know they're asking us not to climb Uluru, and in a way I respect that, because what they're doing is making us take responsibility for doing it.

'But they've said to me, "If the land speaks to you, if the land says yes, who am I to say no?"'

MARLA, MARREE, MARS

The last time I travelled the Oodnadatta Track was in 2000, just after the last big rains. Lake Eyre was full for the first time in an age, and the pub at William Creek was crawling with a plague of stink beetles. You literally couldn't walk without crushing them underfoot. The Track was green then.

This time it's parched and almost devoid of life. For the whole six-hundred-kilometre trip, which included some driving in the early morning and late afternoon, we saw only eight kangaroos, and probably could have counted the crows and kites as well if we'd had a notion to.

Benino has recently done a school assignment on Oodnadatta, so she's looking forward to seeing the place. We stop at the bright pink café and she sees the canoes for hire, no doubt left there to give the tourists something to ponder. But the real irony is when the place floods enough to be able to use the canoes I imagine you'd have to swim to the café to hire them.

Along the way is Anna Creek, the world's largest cattle station, so large that you can fly at two kilometres above it and not see the boundary in any direction. Stock ratio isn't high at the best of times and they normally run about eighteen thousand head. When we passed through we were told they were down to four thousand, and thinking about off-loading more. Later we met a cattle train driver hauling a load from the station to a destination somewhere up the Strzelecki Track, no doubt stock from the last four thousand.

What we did see while flying over the station was an extraordinary amount of dieback in the desert vegetation; at least 50 per cent, perhaps even more. Nature's honest response to drought.

We were flying out from William Creek to see the newest attraction on the map, The Painted Hills, a twenty-kilometre strip of rolling sandstone hills painted every hue from rich ochre to pale yellow. I'm told the sandstone has a high iron content, which oxidises in layers according to the time it's exposed to the air and the percentage of ore it contains, causing a remarkable 'wave and ripple' effect. Like scoops of buttery ice-cream with chocolate, caramel and mulberry swirls.

Not surprisingly, the mining companies have also worked out the area is high in mineral resources, and there's some serious exploration under way right through this region. So I guess the quicker this landmark finds its way onto the mainstream tourist itinerary the better chance it has of being left alone.

Roughly a hundred kilometres to the south, at Roxby Downs, one of our 'big two' miners plans to develop the world's largest open-cut mine. I'm told there'll be an airport large enough to take direct jet flights from all the capital cities, a community of six thousand miners and their families, and enough water to run the whole show stored in the Olympic Dam reservoir, which I'm told will be sourced from the Great Artesian Basin (GAB).

The GAB is the large underground reserve of water trapped in a dish of sandstone beneath much of Queensland, northern New South Wales, south-eastern Northern Territory, and north-eastern South Australia. The water is said to be three thousand metres deep in parts, and conventional wisdom asserts the supply is recharged by surface water slowly filtering in through the layers of sandstone in the Great Divide.

Another school of thought claims the Basin is very much a finite resource, and once we've used the estimated sixty-thousand-odd cubic kilometres of water there will be no more.

What we do know for certain is, since we started tapping into the Basin in the late 1880s, many of the natural mound springs have dried up, and farmers in some parts are reporting a severe drop in water pressure and a need to drill much deeper to reach the supply.

How a mining operation of the aforementioned magnitude will impact on the GAB is something I suspect we'll all be hearing more about as the opening date looms.

On the surface, though, the land hereabouts is as desolate and inhospitable as any in the country. Yet it's still capable of throwing up a surprise.

Talc Alf moved to Lyndhurst for the talc supply more than a decade ago and never left. Since then he's been carving talc tablets and developing his own theories on life, and deciphering the real meaning behind the letters in our alphabet.

'When my daughter was about four years old,' he tells me, 'I started drawing the letters of the alphabet in the sand to get her interested in letters, and it dawned on me the letters were all sculptures. So eventually I worked out the whole English alphabet.'

He is an engaging soul who speaks with an earnestness that's hard to resist. We're talking in his outdoor studio, where he has countless talc sculptures on display, and a blackboard he uses to illustrate his sometimes complex theories.

'To give you an example, Australia starts with *au*,' he tells me, 'which is actually the symbol for gold. And coming towards the west coast of Western Australia – which they call the golden west now – if you were coming from Africa in a sailing boat five hundred years ago, you were heading for *au* the golden, *s* for the sun, *t* for the rising of it, so *aust* is actually east, followed by *ra*, which is the Egyptian name for the sun, where *l* the land, *is*.

'So the whole name *Australis* means "east towards the golden sun where the land is"', he concludes, with a finishing flourish towards his blackboard full of letters and squiggles.

He also shares with me his theory on the origins of Australian Rules football.

'If you look at the start of an Aussie Rules game it's like two big kangaroos lined up against each other to do battle during the mating season,' he reasons. 'And the Aboriginals had a similar game around Melbourne with individual one-on-one contests around the field, like kangaroos, which white man copied and developed from there.

'Whereas rugby and soccer are like the old European games where you get the armies lined up against each other. But Aussie Rules football is a competition between the two individuals, like the kangaroos.'

And I have to admit, the drawing on his blackboard at the end of this theory looked remarkably similar to some of the coaches' game plans I've seen in dressing rooms over the years.

From Talc Alf's we keep heading south, with the country slowly greening up as we approach Adelaide. But it takes many kilometres before we can look out the window and not be reminded of how dry it is.

I guess it's not surprising the issue of water is highlighted here. We've all heard the old cliché about South Australia being the driest state in the driest continent on Earth; the Oodnadatta Track must be up there among the driest places in that state.

And a small point to illustrate South Australians' level of water-awareness: halfway along the Track we went through some roadworks where the boys were busy grading the road and wetting down the dust to keep it settled. Naturally we picked up some mud on the flanks of *The Parrot*, and every day for the next week or so till the mud fell off I was constantly being asked where it came from. It was a shame to see it go.

Just as it was a shame to put Benino on her homeward-bound plane. Last time I couldn't be sure what her selected highlights would be, but this time it was a lot clearer. She would remember the walk up Uluru, flying over the Painted Hills, and perhaps most of all bumping into a certain well-known media personality at the airport. Oh yes, celebrity still rates highly with this ten-year-old.

NUDISTS AND FLIES

Driving around Lake Bonney in South Australia I saw a sign saying 'Nudist Caravan Park – Vacancies', so naturally I went in. I've not seen too many nudist caravan parks in my travels and I thought this might be a good time to ask a few of the more obvious questions.

The proprietor and his wife are gentle, thoughtful souls who welcome me with a cuppa and a ready explanation.

'It's always been a desire of ours to live a naked life,' he tells me. 'And if you were to ask me if I would run a conventional caravan park the answer would be no, because I wouldn't cope well with hordes of people.'

'So who comes to a nudist caravan park?'

'Nudists only make up about 1 per cent of the population,' she explains. 'And of that 1 per cent some join clubs, some only go to the free beaches, and some will come to resorts like this one. So it's really a small demographic to draw from.'

'Are there any specific issues with running a nudist caravan park you wouldn't have with a normal one?'

'Well, only the clothing,' he says. 'We chose not to offer a clothing-optional rule because there are plenty of places for people to camp if they want to wear clothes.'

'And we thought that would probably attract voyeurs and other undesirable elements.'

'But surely if it's cold in the morning you can put something on?'

'Of course! We don't want to have bits falling off and find ourselves running over them with the lawn mower,' she explains, laughing.

It's a warped image I have trouble erasing.

'And do you get many people just dropping in out of curiosity?'

'We got one bloke this morning,' he starts.

'Ah, but I haven't got my kit off,' I say.

'Not yet,' she says, with a smile that makes me cross my legs protectively.

The only guests at the park while I'm there are a couple of entomologists who teach me more about flies than I ever wanted to know.

'When most people talk about flies, they're only talking about bush flies and house flies,' I'm told. 'Because they're the only two species they come across.'

'There may only be two species,' I counter, 'but there are plenty of them.'

'That's the problem,' she says, 'especially in inland Australia, where you can find huge numbers of bush flies. But when you walk inside, they leave you, because they don't like the shade. And the ones you encounter inside are house flies, not bush flies. People don't realise that.'

'You see, we've got something like eight to ten thousand species of flies in Australia that have been described,' he adds. 'And we estimate there's another twelve thousand yet to be described, completely unknown and unnamed.

'In fact we've just been working on some flies from Lamington National Park as big as a speck of dirt; most people wouldn't even see them, but put them under a microscope and they're the most beautiful thing you've ever seen.'

'I believe only an entomologist would say that. And if you're so good at finding them, why can't you disappear them?'

'Well I worked on bush flies for quite a few years at CSIRO in Canberra,' he says. 'And all we found out was that they breed in cattle dung, which the dung beetle was introduced to get rid of, and which it did so successfully that when we had to go bush on a field trip we had to take our own dung. And when I say our own dung I mean our own cattle dung, because as fast as the cows were shitting on the ground the dung beetles were cleaning it up. And there were no bush flies while the dung beetles were active.'

'What about blowflies?'

'Well they're very interesting because they're carrion feeders,' he continues, 'and there are about two species that don't lay eggs but deliver their young live. So you can be sitting there eating your dinner and this particular blowfly will fly past and squirt her maggots straight out from her back end onto your steak.'

'But the thing to remember about maggots is they are very clean animals, and a good source of protein,' she adds. 'And they only eat the decaying flesh, not the live flesh, which is why they've been used in medicine to clean up wounds for hundreds of years.'

'Except for the New Guinea Screw Worm Fly larvae,' he informs me, 'which will eat you alive.'

'And then of course there's the trouser fly,' I suggest helpfully, remembering where I was conducting the interview.

'Yes, but you can zip them up pretty well these days,' he concludes, 'so they're really not much of a problem.'

And I look around the grounds of the well-mown caravan park and marvel at what a great country this is, that I can be conducting an interview with a couple of nudist entomologists on a beautiful spring morning, birds singing, gentle breeze blowing, and not a fly in sight.

Suddenly I cross my legs again.

WATER PLEASE

South Australians are good irrigators, as good as any in the country.

'We've got no choice,' a grape grower from the Riverland tells me. 'We have to make hard decisions and work with the rest of Australia, to ensure we have a future.

'Without water,' he tells me, 'Adelaide would only be 25 per cent of its present size, by population.

'The river Murray supplies 95 per cent of the population of South Australia, which is incredible, and we only have that one river – we have no dams, other than the catchment dam in the Adelaide Hills – so we're reliant on New South Wales and Victoria to supply us with water.

'We've contributed to infrastructure upstream, particularly to the building of the Dartmouth Dam, and we don't care if the majority of federal funding goes to the eastern states, so long as it goes towards fixing up their infrastructure.'

'Are you saying the infrastructure's crook in the eastern states?'

'New South Wales takes seven hundred gigalitres of water to fill their channels before the farmer gets a drop of water. Whereas in South Australia every drop of water that comes out of the river is used on the plant.

'Farming's no longer just a way of life: it's a science. And a lot of the smaller farmers can't afford to keep up, or just haven't got the time or inclination.

'We're only applying the right amount of fertiliser and the right amount of water, when the vine needs it. And I can do all this – measure the moisture content, turn the pump on, even buy and sell parcels of water from anywhere on the system – all from my laptop while I'm a thousand kilometres away fishing.

'Many years ago – just like every other farmer in the region – I used to buy a truckload of "feel good" fertiliser, spread it across the vines, and then we'd water the hell out of it and wash it past the root zone.

'The vines got hardly any benefit,' he concludes. 'The only things that got any benefit were the drains that washed it all into the river. So now I "fertigate" to thirty centimetres, and nothing goes past.'

In brief, there are four main storage reservoirs on the system: the Hume and Dartmouth (aforementioned) Dams; the Menindee Lakes (empty at the time of writing); and Lake Victoria (in New South Wales but controlled by South Australia). There's also the system of locks and weirs along the Murray, which regulates the flow of water and allows passage for boating and facilitates recreational use. And at the mouth of the system there are five barrages constructed primarily to stop the salt water travelling upstream, and to provide storage for service to Adelaide and the south-east of the state.

Historically there's been much debate over how much water came out of the Murray, where and for what purpose, going right back to the 1800s when the river transport operators would fight with the irrigators for reducing the river to a level where the paddle steamers could no longer run (a problem that was mostly resolved with the construction of the weirs).

We've even had eastern state premiers who've publicly stated they didn't care how little water left their western boundary, so long as they were okay for water in their state.

These days the Murray Darling Basin Commission* and various regional water-regulating bodies work towards ensuring everyone gets a fair share of the water, but it's still a juggling act of Herculean proportions, especially with the states still operating unilaterally.

'At the moment Victoria's on zero allocation, but they've been granted 50 per cent of their carry-over, which means they will have some water,' the chief executive of one of the regional regulators told me earlier on the trip. 'In South Australia they're on 4 per cent of their allocation, and in New South Wales they're on zero allocation; they're just providing critical-needs water to stock and permanent plantings, and big employers.'

'So there are still definitely anomalies in the system,' she admits. 'The federal government is trying to get the three states to comply with the one set of guidelines, but until that happens we'll continue to see the kind of scenario I just painted, with South Australia, Victoria and New South Wales doing completely different things with the same amount of water.

'What we need is a drive from the federal government to enforce a consistent approach to usage, so if you're a permanent planter in one state you don't get less water than your counterpart in another.'

My Riverland irrigator echoes a similar sentiment.

'It's not the farmers' fault: it's the politicians,' he asserts. 'I've spoken to those farmers in the eastern states and they're just the same as South Australian growers, they all want to do the right thing. They're the sons and grandsons of the guys who fought and died at Gallipoli with our forefathers. We talk the same language, we're the same people.'

Yes, South Australians are fine irrigators, no doubt. But perhaps they're even better negotiators.**

* Now the Murray Darling Basin Authority

** The National Water Plan was, indeed, implemented by the incoming Labor government, but it seems the gun negotiator was the Victorian premier who demanded a lazy billion to commit, because he argued successfully that he'd already put his irrigators through more pain than the two northern states, and any benefit to Victoria's irrigation system would improve South Australia's as well – precisely the point my Riverland irrigator was making.

CLANCY LIVES

Driving up the Lachlan Valley in central New South Wales, I come across a drover running about four or five hundred head of the fattest cattle I've seen all trip, so I stop for a yarn.

He's a big bloke with a ruddy face and a beaming smile, but he's a bit rattled at present because he's just run over one of his dogs, which is not looking too good lying in the back of the ute.

'I think I might've busted him inside, bugger it,' he says. 'He's a good little pup, too, that one. Just came runnin' out of the mob not lookin' and straight under the wheels.'

He tells me he'd normally be working from horseback, only the equine flu virus has meant he's had to send his horses back home for a spell.

'Wouldn'ta happened if I'd had me horses. Bugger.'

The pup's on his side and trying hard to raise his head when he hears his master's voice. He's not whimpering, and doesn't yelp when the drover lifts the pup's back leg to feel the break in it. The pup puts his head back down with a little sigh as if resigned to his lot.

The drover invites me to share some dinner with him and his wife, and tells me to head back to his camp while he puts the mob in the reserve for the night.

He's camped under a stand of trees just off the road, and his setup consists of a big, old caravan he pulls behind a sturdy-looking truck, a couple of trailers and a sulky strapped to the back of the last of them.

I'm greeted by half a dozen dogs tied up and going crook, and the drover's wife, who in contrast accepts the arrival of a complete stranger driving a loudly decorated campervan as if it were the most usual of bush happenings.

We talk a bit and she tells me they're from the Riverina country and she's only up for a visit for a couple of days. She used to be on the road full time with her husband – in fact they raised five kids on the road – but she reckons she's retired these days, and prefers life back home.

I imagine their daughters would make hardy wives with a rearing like that.

The drover returns directly and puts the pup in a trailer on his own.

'I don't like his chances,' he says to me, and you can tell he's about as cut up as a drover ever gets about one of his dogs. There's no place for sentiment when it comes to working dogs; they don't even pat them, as a rule. And if you do they'll likely tell you not to go spoiling their dog.

Over dinner and a few red wines he tells me he's been droving pretty much all his life, right through New South Wales and a good chunk of Queensland too.

'Things have changed a lot,' he says. 'Bit too much bureaucracy now.'

He explains how the Rural Lands Protection Board controls the licensing for the Travelling Stock Routes, and about the penalty fees for going too slow.

'But sometimes you don't worry about that if there's good feed about. The stock's gotta come first, second and third. My job's to hand these cattle back to their owners in better condition than when I got 'em.'

He's obviously proud of his work and his reputation as a good drover, but he speaks with a lot of humility, and most times when he makes a point he'll refer to his wife for her view. He's not a highly educated man, but it's clear he's done a lot of thinking about things.

'Met a lot of good people on the road,' he says. 'My word, yes. And a few not so good.

'In fact they nearly did me in a few years back. Yeah. Got accused of cattle rustlin', just because the stock was in good shape.

'Opened the door of the caravan one mornin' and there was the Stock Squad cops with guns pointed at me; they had helicopters, and men everywhere ... the whole show.

'All because I look after me cattle. They reckoned I must have pinched 'em. How they figure a bloke could steal fifteen hundred head of cattle while he's drovin' down the long paddock, in full view of everybody, I got no idea.

'You can't do nothin' out here without everybody knowin'. They'd know where you camped last night, where you are now. It's not like the city.

'Sure, we're always lookin' for a killer, a stray that's bolted when it's come off the truck. But I'd no more pinch a man's cattle than ...'

He turns his hands upward. Then he turns his palms down and puts them on the table.

'Almost got too much for me at one point. Just about ready to shoot meself.'

His wife's been busying herself cooking dinner while we've been talking, often chiming in with a comment or two. At this last statement she makes no contribution, no sign she even heard it. But it's surely a subject she knows well and with prompting she joins in, and together they tell me the full story. Not for a proud drover and his wife to avoid the truth of it, whatever it is.

In short he got himself wrapped up so tight trying to defend his innocence against the rustling charges that he lost the plot. He doesn't remember the final stages – didn't even remember where he was, and had to describe the landmarks in the countryside over the phone so his wife could work out where to send a daughter to collect him – he only remembers that his family rallied. Then they spelled him for a bit and now he's back, good as new. Maybe a little more circumspect, but I'm guessing that bit.

I ask him how the people are coping with the drought.

'These towns are sufferin', no doubt about it. But I was only talkin' to a bloke yesterday, who was tellin' me that what you see in the towns now, the people still hangin' in, they'll be there at the end.'

'Is this the worst one you've ever seen?' I ask him.

'Yeah this is the worst I've seen. I was only thinkin' today, I wonder how tough it can really get. We reckon it's bad now, but how'd the old fellas go back when they had to cart their own water?

'Wouldn't be twenty kilometres from here they drowned about two hundred and fifty head of bullocks rushing the water because they hadn't had a drink for days. Well that don't happen no more, because we've got tankers to cart water for a thousand head.

'And they had the rabbits to compete with. We don't have rabbits like them days.

'We got plenty of feed. We've got this stuff you can put in the water to feed the bug in the cows guts so they can go for a long time without much to eat, so we can keep 'em alive in the heat.

'Yeah, it's a bit rough at the moment. But once we get over it, this country'll produce.

'We just want rain.'

And I was humbled by the thinking of the man, who, in the middle of the worst drought he'd ever seen, preferred to think himself lucky he had it so much better than his predecessors.

In the morning his pup was up on three legs, wagging his tail and looking like he was going to tough it out as well.

I had written him a letter, which I had for want of better
Knowledge, sent to where I met him down the Lachlan years ago
He was shearing when I knew him so I sent the letter to him
Just on spec, addressed as follows, Clancy of the Overflow

Banjo Patterson, 'Clancy of the Overflow'

FAMILIES AND FERALS

My old man and I don't always recollect events the same way. When he remembers the flying dinghy incident he refers to it as: 'That time you pinched the boat off the roof of the car without my knowledge.'

So we're returning to the scene of my crime to see how the Macquarie Marshes are faring in the drought.

When it's full, the Marshes are a haven for birdlife and all manner of swamp creature. On that last trip we made thirty years ago, the Macquarie was in flood, and we discovered nesting Red-necked Crakes at the northern end of the Marshes, a bird well out of its known habitat. That discovery has been something of a sticking point for my father, because it seems no-one else in the world saw them on the Marshes that year, or any other year for that matter, and he wants it recognised.

We meet at Warren and plan to travel up to the Red-necked Crakes' nursery the next day, dropping in on the scene of the 'great dinghy theft' just for old times' sake along the way.

That night, my father's wife, who loves to tell stories about my father's misadventures, tells me the latest.

It seems they had this old sheep at home, which was getting more and more decrepit with every day. Fearing he would be soon digging a big hole to bury the animal, my father negotiated a swap with one of his distant neighbours for a goat with gammy horns. It was a clean swap, the old sheep for the much younger-looking (albeit uglier) goat, effective immediately.

Unfortunately the goat dropped dead within a week of arriving at my father's house. Meanwhile the old sheep lives on, contentedly grazing in his new paddock.

He's a winner, my old man, no question. And he digs a good hole, too.

The next morning we drove up the western flank of the Marshes. We were expecting it to be dry and if anything our expectations were exceeded. There was very little water in the river, and none evident in the Marshes.

I had been told in town that a good environmental flow had been earmarked for the Marshes, but it was hard to imagine any amount making much of a difference, even if it could find its way through all the 'black snakes' (irrigation pipes). There'd been a well-publicised water theft earlier in the year that had drawn attention to just how dire the situation was.

Cattle were grazing where the swamp used to be waist deep, and you could barely recognise the area where we found the Red-necked Crakes' nests all those years ago. If my father expected any evidence of the misplaced Crakes to be still remaining, he was in for a disappointment, and the realisation that I was now his only witness, living or material, must have filled him with dismay.

'I don't know where I went wrong with you, son,' he'd often say when I'd fail to remember things as he did. 'You showed so much promise when you were young.'

But not all things suffer in times of drought and, according to a local fox shooter I catch up with, some of the ferals were having a field day.

'Not so much the rabbits,' he tells me, 'but the pigs and the foxes are doin' real well. The foxes are eating the dead lambs, and feeding off the sheep carcasses. And the farmers are handfeeding the sheep with oats and wheat or whatever, and the wild pigs come out at night and eat the grain trails. But you don't see so many rabbits about at the moment.'

'What about the roo shooters?' I ask. 'How are they going?'

'Not real good in the Warren area. Yeah, the roos have either moved on, or been shot out, but they're as scarce as I've ever seen 'em here.'

'So it's really just the opportunistic feeders, the pigs and foxes that are thriving?'

'Yeah. And the pigs are real smart, you know, and they'll drink from the sheep's water trough, and eat their feed. And I've seen 'em feeding on the fox carcasses I've left in a heap. Foxes'll eat their own carcasses as well. They'll eat just about anything, from grasshoppers and frogs and lizards, to dead lambs, and afterbirth.'

'So sheep don't eat their own afterbirth like cows do?'

'Yeah, that's a sight, isn't it? But sheep don't, no. So the foxes eat them. Don't know how many live lambs they get, though. The cockies say they get a few, but I've never seen a fox taking a lamb.'

'So how many foxes do you get a night?'

'Anywhere between ten and forty, usually. And there seems to be the same number comin' back every year. The ten-eighty baits don't seem to do a lot of good. I've been onto properties that have been baited with ten-eighty a month before, and still shot forty foxes.'

He uses a Remington .17 calibre rifle, and changes the barrel almost every year. He brings out a magazine with an article about himself and a photo of the shooter surrounded by fox pelts. He tells me there's no real money in it these days, like there was back when he could sell the pelts for thirty dollars each. Now the farmer supplies him with a bit of diesel, and he only gets about ten dollars a pelt, he says it's more of a winter hobby than a real job. He's a builder by trade and he reckons if he wasn't foxing he'd be doing nothing at the moment.

'Yeah, I'd feel like I was letting the farmers down if I didn't do it now,' he says. 'Whenever I show 'em a pile of foxes I've shot on their property, they can't stop shaking my hand. That's why I keep doin' it, I guess. For the farmers. They got enough on their hands without havin' to worry about foxes and pigs, too.'

NOT APPLES IN ORANGE

Orange is not one of my favourite destinations.

It is the scene of another mainland co-broadcast with Charlie – from the National Field Days – and while we're there we stay with a couple of his friends. They're fine country folk, and generous to a fault, so I decide it would be a nice gesture to cook them dinner and give them a break for our last night.

A barbeque is agreed on, some quality fillet is found, along with chats and salad and fresh bread rolls, and since I've volunteered, I am to be at the controls. Normally this wouldn't be a risky proposition, since I'm a fair cook, but a funny thing happened on the way to the forum.

To begin with, since I'm in such a benevolent mood I also suggest we take our hosts from the radio station out for a few drinks beforehand. It would, I argue, be bad form not to. So we do. And it's in good form I return to cook dinner.

The first sign of trouble comes when I'm introduced to the barbeque, an enormous, arrogant-looking thing that almost spoke the words, 'One false move and I'll torch everything, including you.' I feel so intimidated I gulp down half my wine.

Then my host offers me a set of barbeque utensils so large I think they're a joke, but as I'm about to burst into laughter I notice he's stroking the utensils with some kind of weird reverence. I take a deep breath and another slug of my wine.

But with a little help here and there I get a few salads organised, chats steamed, and steak and sausages on and sizzling. Everything is under control. I celebrate with a refill. Life is good.

Then it all comes undone, and like the final moments before a car crash I watch it unfold as if I am the innocent bystander I wish I was.

First comes the realization I've forgotten someone's pineapple ring but before I can correct this terrible oversight the hostess wants to know if there's a sausage ready now because people are starving to death and don't forget she likes her steak really well done so I prod the thing and raise my glass to show I'm onto it and rush inside for the pineapple but when I return the snags are on fire I guess that means they're about ready and someone wants heated bread God give me a break in this day and age heated bread then someone else shouts "Plates!" as if they've just discovered gold and people are running everywhere with cutlery and condiments barking orders and really how do they expect an artist to work in this environment and I plate up the meat burnt side down and present the steaming chats tossed in butter and parsley to the host but his face drops like he's having a stroke and I'm momentarily confused thinking he might be joking but then he gives me the same *these giant utensils are the only kind real men use* look I got before and I remember he wanted 'potato bake' God don't worry about the break just give me another drink and now her steak's not done well enough and she's playing it for an academy award and Charlie observes I am like Badger in *Wind in the Willows* come out of his burrow but I feel more like Toad of Toad Hall when the world just isn't turning as it should.

I think it's fair to say it isn't one of my finer performances.

COOKIE MONSTERS

Well, they're still doing drugs up Nimbin way. And the streets are still a freak show and the buildings psychedelic gauche. Yep, it looks for all the world like the hippies got away with it.

By the end of 1960s the northern New South Wales town of Nimbin was almost dead. Dairy was all but finished and bananas were going the same way. The tiny strip of shops in the main street was ailing and there seemed to be no remedy in sight.

Cue the hippies. Following the tide created by the Woodstock music festival in 1969, a groundswell of students and alternative lifestylers decided to hold a festival in Nimbin to celebrate the dawning of the Age of Aquarius.

When they came, the hippies brought with them peace, love and marijuana; they painted the town joyous, threw away their inhibitions and settled in to make the most of the easy climate and naturally beautiful surroundings. Nimbin was saved.

And somehow, unlike Byron Bay, Port Douglas and the Daintree, among other places that can also boast a strong 'alternative' history, Nimbin has managed to hang on to its heady roots. Perhaps the coastal haunts were always destined to fall to the developers because the settings were just too beautiful to be held, and Nimbin's off-Broadway location and inherent dagginess proved a solid defence, I don't know. But it seems the hippies have secured the town's identity and, just like Kings Cross in Sydney is now as much a tourist attraction as it is a sex precinct, Nimbin's fame as a drug haunt for ferals is rivalled only by its reputation as a stopover for tourists coming to see what all the fuss is about.

And coming to buy pot, of course. Of all towns in Australia, Nimbin enjoys the most freedom when it comes to buying and selling marijuana publicly. Transactions are commonplace and conducted almost openly on the street. Indeed, about the only way you can walk down the main street and not get offered dope is if you look like a cop.

Sure they've had their share of problems with harder drugs, and recently council even installed surveillance cameras to help keep an eye on street dealing, but ostensibly Nimbin's a pot town. And quasi-legal hippy-trippy stuff like Philosopher's Stone and other psychoactive herbal drugs you can buy over the counter at any one of the specialty shops in the main street.

Philosopher's Stone is an hallucinogenic, which comes from a truffle-like growth at the base of a magic mushroom. Legally it enjoys a certain ambiguous status, since it's not illegal to pick and use a magic mushroom, or indeed to give it to someone else for their use. It only becomes an illegal substance when it's altered by human hand for sale or profit.

The way retailers circumvent this issue is by recommending an alternate use of the substance at the point of sale.

'Philosopher's Stone sold for the purpose of burning as incense, for example, is perfectly legal,' the proprietor of one such shop tells me.

While I'm talking to her a couple of young men from Melbourne approach the counter to buy some. They listen carefully to her explanation of what would happen if the 'incense' was accidentally ingested, and seem slightly disappointed to learn that the side effects would only last five hours.

I ask the lads why they don't just go for a wander out in the paddocks and find some magic mushies for free, rather than pay sixty dollars a hit for Philosopher's Stone. There'd been recent rain so there was likely to be a few Gold Tops about.

'I dunno,' one of the guys tells me. 'This is easier. And we know what we're getting.'

'Is this your first time?'

'No, we come up all the time. Whenever we can.'

I ask his mate what they get up to when they're wasted on Philosopher's Stone and he says, 'Not much. Sit around and laugh our heads off, mostly.'

Fair enough.

I wander back up the street and slip into the Nimbin Museum. With the brief background I've already given you I'm sure you can imagine the kind of paraphernalia on display, but it's well worth a visit.

While I'm there a young bloke opens up a big bag of marijuana heads and asks me if I want some. I ask him if it's locally grown.

'Reckon so. Best heads in town, man. You want?'

I thank him and decline. It's been a long time since I was interested in that sort of caper, though I admit I used to be quite partial to sitting around laughing my head off back in the old days.

But it's not only the recreational users who come to Nimbin to source drugs. The use of marijuana as a pain killer is widely known, and a growing number of elderly people are now using it as their treatment of choice. And since it's readily available on the streets of Nimbin, it's a logical inclusion to many a Grey Nomad's itinerary.

I ask a café owner what would happen if the police stumbled into a dope transaction between a dealer and a Grey Nomad.

'Well, to begin with that would only happen if both parties didn't see each other first,' he tells me. 'Because if they did the policeman probably wouldn't walk that way, and the gear would get hidden, and they'd each look the other way.

'Frankly I've never heard of anyone getting busted like that. It'd be fairly embarrassing for a twenty-year-old cop to be booking a sixty-five-year-old grandmother for selling a few cookies to another sixty-five-year-old grandmother.'

'So it's mainly cookies they buy?'

'Yeah. Sometimes they buy smoking pot and take it home to make their own. But mostly they buy their cookies here.'

The same guy was approached by the state government some years back to conduct experimental trials in the production of marijuana, with a view to developing a strain suitable for medicinal use, but the idea was ultimately shelved.

'Primarily they decided it would be sending out the wrong message to legalise it. But the larger drug companies put a lot of pressure on as well.'

'How did they come to choose you?'

'I don't know. They just thought I could help,' he says, chuckling a little at his own drollery and having another toke on his joint.

'We were already trialling a low-THC*-level hemp crop on the same farm, so I guess I was an obvious choice. The crop went well, too. Then the drought hit and everything on the black soil plains died. But I'm pleased to say the hemp was the last to go. Just another two inches of rain and we'd have scraped through.'

'So you'd recommend hemp as a drought-resistant crop?'

'Well it did better than the wheat. And even what we grew we could have used for silage if the licence had allowed it, you know, to feed to the cows.'

'Are cows affected by the THC in the plant?' I ask him.

'I don't know. I've never smoked with a cow,' he tells me, not entirely deadpan.

'But I did hear of a dog, recently,' he continues, 'that found a few cookies and ate them. And he wouldn't get up, wouldn't do anything, and because his owners didn't know he'd got the cookies they thought he might have been bitten by a snake, so they took him to the vet.

'But the vet had seen it before and knew exactly what it was. So he just told them to give the dog a Mars bar and a milkshake and he'd be right as rain.'

Boom - tish.

And even though they're still doing the same old gags up here I find it hard not to have a soft spot for the place. Indeed, for a brief moment I even contemplated seeing what a dose of Philosopher's Stone could teach me now, just for old time's sake. But I suspect it wouldn't be anything I don't already know.

Instead I think I'll leave all that to the backpackers who come by the busload every day from Byron Bay, and settle on a smile whenever I think of how the old hippies got away with it after all.

* THC – Tetrahydrocannabinol: the active constituent in cannabis.

THE SIXTH EXTINCTION

A couple of weeks before I went through Lismore they had the king of all hail storms, which broke a squillion windows in cars and houses alike and caused enough damage to the town for it to be declared a natural disaster zone. Eyewitnesses reported a residue of hail stones left in the street half a metre deep, some the size of grapefruits, and everywhere I looked I saw cars heavily pockmarked with dints.

The weekend I was there a mini-tornado monstered the small town of Dunoon, just north of Lismore, blowing away a campervan in the process. It could have been me, flying away in *The Parrot*.

On the Sunday the region around Beaudesert, just over the border in Queensland, got belted by another wild storm.

And the Christmas–New Year period saw constant flooding in north-eastern New South Wales and south-eastern and central Queensland, setting new rainfall records and producing yet more natural disaster zones.

And this is just one tiny little pocket of one country in the space of two months.

Worldwide natural disasters are becoming commonplace, and many believe this is due in no small part to climate change. And while still a contentious issue, most scientists are in agreement this cycle of change is largely the result of human activity.*

A palaeobotanical love story heightens my awareness.

He was an Australian cattle farmer with an interest in geology and plants, who gained acceptance into the scientific community by writing a number of significant papers on the subject.

She was a South African student who came to Australia on a field trip, when he invited her to his home to see his collection of fossils, his etchings, as it were.

It took some time, mind you, and life had a few twists and turns for both in that time, but the Aussie farmer with the enquiring mind and the bright young scientist from the land of the proteas did eventually get together.

And in many ways the protea was responsible for their union, for it was the widespread distribution of the protea family of plants (known chiefly as banksia and grevillea in Australia) that helped convince scientists that the Southern Hemisphere continents (plus a large chunk of the subcontinent) once formed a great land mass now recognised as Gondwana. And it was the fossilised forebears of these (among other) plants on their two continents in particular that had drawn her to Australia.

'So we've had a long palaeobotanical connection,' he tells me, laughing. 'It was a bit like Gondwana getting back together.'

And about as likely, it seems to me. Like a love letter written in mud and left for a hundred million years for the intended recipients to find by chance.

I ask what it is about palaeobotany that excites her. When she speaks she does so in a beautiful South African accent, unlike any other I've ever heard from that country. From her mouth the flattened vowel sounds so characteristic of South African speech were soft and supple, as if being delivered on a pillow, with not a trace of harshness.

'I just though it was so exciting,' she tells me, 'that you could know about ancient floras, that you could have a look at what was preserved in the rocks and just from a few fossil leaves you could say what kind of a plant they came from, what kind of climate they lived in.'

'Do you think we can we learn anything from the past?' I ask.

'Ah this is a big question,' he says. 'There've been catastrophes in the past. At the end of the Permian period, which is when all the major coal measures in the Southern Hemisphere were formed, there was a catastrophic extinction event, which wiped out over

90 per cent of all living organisms on Earth.

'And we're all more familiar with the end of the Cretaceous period, when there was probably a meteor impact that changed the whole atmospheric conditions and wiped out the dinosaurs. All except for the birds.

'But I think the worrying thing is that one animal on Earth is creating the next catastrophe. And I think mankind is going to wreak havoc in the very near future with his past actions of multiplying and being so materialistic, using up all the Earth's resources.

'I think maybe man will be remembered for creating the Sixth Extinction on Earth. Only there'll be nobody around to see it.'

'Does it ever get too much for you to comprehend?' I ask. 'Do you ever feel like lying down and letting the mud flow over you?'

'Well I think it'd be wonderful to become a fossil, and whatever creatures are around in a few million years would split open a rock, and there I would be. That would be a wonderful way to go.'

* I'm aware of the contrary arguments, in particular those that have proliferated since the recent cooling trend has been documented. However, at this point in time I believe the evidence still weighs heavily in favour of the stance taken above.

THE NEW KID

There is a new breed of farmer infiltrating the bush. He has money. He has energy. He doesn't need to make a living from the land; rather, he seeks the lifestyle it offers. He is not disillusioned.

He comes from the city, from a successful career, and brings with him a wife and young children. They come to the country for a gentler life, a rural experience, a tree change.

They enrol their kids in the local school and sign them up to the swimming club. They join the tennis association and buy a small business in town, or perhaps continue to run a scaled-down version of their city practice from their new home. And their new home will be on a farm, of course.

They will buy this farm in a run-down condition and upgrade. All the things the previous owner never quite managed they will address. Fences will be replaced, pastures improved, homesteads renovated, and the land will be stocked with the best that money can buy.

They may not stay on the land forever, and might choose to move back to the city to educate their kids, but while they're there they will inject much-needed funds into the regions they choose. Not to mention optimism.

I have a friend who roughly fits this bill. He was in real estate when I knew him and, not surprisingly, when he went bush he bought well. Now he's sitting on an investment that has exceeded all growth expectations in any market. He has reason to gloat, yet he doesn't.

'Nice piece of land you've got here, mate,' I say.

'Yeah, it's not bad.'

The great Australian understatement.

He takes me on the tour of the property and I notice all the new fencing going in is timber, not wire.

'He's [the fencer] costing me thousands. Tallow wood. It'll be around long after you and I are gone.'

His cattle are all pedigreed Angus and the paddocks are weed-free, or almost. 'Bit of Wild Tobacco, and the Fireweed's a constant battle,' he says. 'But we're winning.' I guess he's got a weed-controller comes in once a month.

He shows me the second farmhouse they've just finished renovating. It sits on its own title with a hundred acres of land, and has a valley view almost as breathtaking as the one from their house. The renovation would have cost plenty, and he tells me they could sell off that block now and pay for the whole farm, but they might as well keep it.

'Might turn it into a bed and breakfast,' he says.

Back home he's got two littluns and a wife obviously enjoying the country lifestyle with no financial constraints.

That night we eat a meal that wouldn't be bettered in a fine city café, and wash it down with quality wine from the cellar. Then we watch music videos on an enormous flat-screen television with surround-sound audio. I sleep in a guest room worthy of any upmarket country hotel.

In the morning over pancakes for breakfast (it's Tuesday) they tell me the only real drawback is the isolation.

'Mainly for the kids, you know. No other kids around here to play with,' she says.

'And I miss the surf,' he admits.

'I've got a few nice friends,' she tells me. 'But we don't have much in common with the real locals, the born-and-bred ones.'

And while they're my friends I can't help feeling they've got one foot in and one foot out, that they could bail out any time they choose, while the 'real locals' are probably doing their best just to hang on. It's no wonder they've little in common.

RED IN THE CENTRE

I took a break over Christmas because it would have been un-Australian not to.

Santa came and went, and my father had his seventy-fifth birthday so we threw him a party. It was the first time the immediate family had been together for many years.

He made a short and uncharacteristically serious speech to the gathering – which included sundry wives, children, grandchildren and friends – and said he had no life regrets except perhaps making a bigger deal of some things than he should have, and not mending a few fences he could have before it was too late.

Christ only knows what the women in his life made of that, but I've always loved this vulnerability in my father, the willingness to allow his failures to show. And I've no doubt it's helped shape who I am. Some people have role models who teach them how to win at all cost; I had one who taught me there's no shame in losing because somebody has to do it. Consequently I've never let a lack of ability or preparation stand in the way of opportunity.

So I began the working year in *The Parrot* at the Tamworth Country Music Festival, where I was booked to perform at the Australia Day concert in the park. In effect it was my first serious gig as a musician, supporting Joe Camilleri and the Black Sorrows before a crowd of ten thousand, but I thought it prudent not to trouble the organisers with this minor detail.

The gig came about because I was asked to MC the event and I accepted on the proviso that I be allowed to play a few of my own songs while I was at it. The organisers agreed and I died a thousand deaths. I had played to numbers before, but without too much effort I could probably have named them all.

For the uninitiated, Tamworth is the home of country music in Australia, and has a Big Guitar to prove it – surely one of the tackiest roadside attractions in the country. It's right up there with the Big Spud at Robertson, New South Wales, which looks like a blind mullet, and the Big Peanut in Atherton, Queensland, which looks like a blind mullet with a face. The Golden Guitar looks nothing like a blind mullet but it does look too surreal to be there and, since that much is indisputable, too real not to have strings.

Incidentally, why Tamworth is the country music capital when the bulk of the recording industry is on the Central Coast of New South Wales I have no idea. I once asked a couple of country artists why everyone hung out on the Central Coast and they told me it was because Tamworth didn't have any decent beaches. Of course.

But I digress. I'm playing Tamworth and I've got a new guitar for the occasion. It's not big or golden, but it is a Fender Telecaster, as bona fide an 'axe' as they come. Dylan played one on his Australian tour in 1966, Harrison played one at the Beatles' last concert in 1969, Keith Richards plays one; only problem is I've never played one. Never played any sort of electric guitar, in fact, and I don't get the thing till two days before the event, a stunt I doubt you'll find in the How to Prepare for a Gig Guide.

Another small concern I've got is I've landed in Tamworth with only half a band. Though it sounded like a good idea before we left, to pick up players once we got here – 'No worries,' my producer said. 'The place is crawling with them.' – in truth, it isn't so easy to find a lead and a bass guitarist prepared to learn three new songs in a hurry and play them in front of a big crowd.

But after some dedicated pub crawling, watching bands and considering every possible combination from fiddle and accordion to keyboard and kazoo (okay, we were getting desperate), we finally find a couple of guitarists who can loosely fit the bill. The catch is they can only give us an hour of rehearsal.

And it's during that brief rehearsal that the band pick up an inflammatory lyric in 'Red in the Centre' and advise me to tone it down or expect a riot.

For the record, the song is a slightly ironic anthem I wrote to highlight some of the issues encountered on the trip, presented in the character of a good old Anglo-Aussie dad who believes 'she'll be right, mate', whatever the reality. The lyric in question is race related, and heard out of context it could certainly sound offensive.

Now some of the boys are telling me if the lyric's staying they're going. I argue that in order to make the point it needs to be sharp, but they seem less concerned about making statements than getting speared on stage, the pussies, so I agree to compromise and tone down the lyric.

Whether it's an advantage or not to be the MC as well as one of the acts is questionable. I guess in one way it helps because I've already built up a rapport with the audience by the time I have to make the transition; but on the flip side they have to make just as much of a transition as me, since they've got me figured as one thing and now I'm strapping on a guitar to become another.

And it's with these thoughts in mind that I give my new Tele a final tune and walk onstage with the boys. What could be so hard about playing a few songs to a big crowd? All I need is a good start to the set and everything will be all right on the night, won't it? Of course it will. Sure it will. How could it possibly go wrong?

So I step up to the mike and take a deep breath and face the crowd then hit the first chord hard to show I mean business and promptly blow my own head off since I've forgotten to turn down my levels after tuning and I glance around to see if I've dropped any of the band and notice the bass player is sitting on his arse Christ I've killed the poor bastard but then I remember he did that so he can read his chord chart thank God someone's on track because I can hear my new rhythm guitarist playing a song I don't remember writing and I'm not entirely sure I'm playing anything I've written either maybe this new guitar just doesn't have the right chords on it and my mouth is dry and I'm sweating so much I can't see out of either eye and I'm thinking aha that's what the bandana thing is all about and the crowd is a mother quietly urging her son to be the best damn soldier in the war and die if you will just don't come home a coward but I'm wishing there was someone else up on stage I could nod to as if to say *you take it from here I'll meet you at the end* but there is only me there is only me unfortunately for everybody there is only me.

Thankfully audiences are forgiving by nature and they politely ignore the shaky start, warm to the second song, and show some genuine appreciation for 'Red'. All things considered, it isn't nearly as messy as it could have been, and no spears are thrown.

There is one sensitive whitefella who finds 'the lyric' still too close to the bone and makes his point after the show and in the local newspaper later in the week, but overall the little song conceived in response to the Australia I saw going around the country was delivered without major hiccup on Australia Day, and 'Red in the Centre' is born.

AND WHEN IT RAINS ...

Even the near-witless chook knows which way is up when its life depends on it. In northern New South Wales a woman tells me she heard a rumble and looked outside in time to see a great chunk of hillside slide down the gully, taking the chook pen with it. By the time she arrived, the pen was buried in mud and slush, with only a small corner exposed to the air where all the chooks were huddled and going crook at the world for this terrible fright. Her son had to cut the wire mesh to free the birds.

The woman's frightened as well. She's a newcomer to the district and she never realised floods could be so devastating.

'My brother drove straight up from Newcastle when he heard how bad things were,' she tells me, her voice full of emotion, 'and he lost his car.

'He got to Kyogle and decided he needed a sleep after the drive, before coming out here. And he woke up at about two in the morning surrounded by water. So he had to wait five hours in his car for the SES to get him out.'

When it really floods up here, houses are washed away and lives are lost. Cars are almost always a casualty.

In fact I'm talking to this woman because I found a newish utility washed down a creek bed. The water had dropped and the stream running beneath the vehicle looked an unlikely culprit, but the smashed windscreen and the side dented against the tree trunk told a different story. Clothes were hung over a nearby fence as if the driver had to swim for safety, then stripped out of his wet clobber before hoofing it home in his underclothes. So I wandered up to the nearest house to find out the story.

'He stalled on the flooded causeway,' the woman tells me. 'So he just put some rocks behind it and left it there, thinking it'd be all right. He didn't think the water would rise as quickly or as high as it did.'

She makes no mention of whether he came home in his underpants, and she is still so shocked by events I think it prudent not to ask.

Kyogle is a town used to flooding. Indeed, I'm told the recent one only ranked as a one-in-twenty-five-year occurrence, a full metre below the last big one in1954, and even that one wasn't the worst they'd seen.

Everywhere you look there's evidence: fences draped in dead grass like kilometres of skinny brown washing hanging on the line; plastic-wrapped bales of hay left stranded by the roadside after floating over the fence while the water was up; and the stench of stale mud heavy on the air.

But not everyone finds the flooding a worry.

A couple of cockies I meet on the way back seem to consider it an interesting diversion, an opportunity for neighbours to compare notes from either side of a swollen creek and go for a swim in the swirling brown water.

'Yeah, all our neighbours didn't miss out on the rapids while they were runnin',' the youngest of the cockies tells me. 'But I'm gettin' too fat these days; I hit every rock on the way down, so I had to give that up.'

So I ask him what his flood highlights are now he's retired from shooting rapids.

'Makin' pikelets for the kids. Watchin' videos. And the picture of the Aboriginal kid jumping off the Casino bridge with a boogie board was pretty funny. All we could see was his two white feet and his board. It was on the back page of the paper with a big caption "This is Not a Sport!"' He erupts into laughter.

Another local I meet is an amateur meteorologist, and he agrees floods are nothing to be scared of providing you use common sense.

'I've got no worries about swimming in the floodwaters,' he says. 'But I grew up here so it's no big deal for me.

'It did come funny this last flood; the river was up and down and up, and we went from expecting a standard flood to one about six or seven feet higher in quick time.

'People mostly get in trouble when they don't really believe it's going to happen, and don't prepare for it.'

But the service station owners in town have to prepare because they both go under, and if they don't seal the fuel tanks the result can be disastrous.

'Yeah, we just unbolt the pumps,' one owner tells me, 'and put a lot of grease under the caps, then seal it down and it's right. I'm pretty good at it these days.'

I tell him that's just as well, because I've been told it's going to rain forever.

'Yeah, I know. We've gone from continual drought to everlasting flood. I've got cattle at home, and six months ago I'd have killed for the feed I've got now. Now I'm mowing the grass.'

'You didn't lose any cattle in the flood?'

'No, I was lucky. One bloke lost nine hundred head. And found them all alive and well down the river. Another fella in town here woke up to find somebody's cow standing in his backyard.'

'It's a wonder more don't drown,' I say.

'Cows do that on purpose, you know. They fill themselves up with air and float around intentionally.'

'You're taking the piss. They're the dumbest animals on Earth.'

'No, they're not. They're smarter than a lot of people walkin' round. I swear it; they fill up with air on purpose.'

And the rain kept coming. Not enough to flood the plains again, but enough to keep the rivers swollen and the frogs vocal. Underfoot the ground stayed wet, casual water lay in puddles all over, and everywhere cattle grazed knee deep in new grass.

And I watched those cattle for any signs of deep breathing; but nothing. Either they knew the worst was over, or it's a secret they don't like to reveal to a stranger.

PUBLIC PRIVACY

It's the people you meet, always the people.

I'm in the Border Ranges region of northern New South Wales, where the floodplains are ever lush and the green hills are often wrapped in a blanket of morning mist.

Public roads in these parts are mostly interconnected, but sometimes only as 'paper roads' on council maps, which weave their way through private property before linking up with other roads in adjacent valleys.

Yesterday I was enjoying a pleasant morning walk along one such road when a man challenged me. I was already at yelling distance past his home when he caught my attention, and wanted to know where I came from and what I was doing.

When I told him, he suggested I might like to use another road for the purpose in future, or else he'd be inclined to set the dogs onto me.

I thanked him for his hospitality and carried on.

But, as I walked back to *The Parrot*, camped at the house of some friends nearby, I decided to return as soon as possible to discuss the matter of road ownership with him. In my mind I was breaking no law of trespassing, since the road was flagged with a regulation-issue council signpost and, although it did eventually become a barely visible 'paper road' and run off through his fenced property, where I was walking it was still very much open slather.

So I returned to fetch the microphone.

Now, when I'm undertaking an assignment that carries with it a degree of tension, shall we say, I always find it wise to wear my most genial manner. This way I have a chance of disarming my target with affability before he has a chance to respond otherwise. Wherever possible I will also take along the largest sidekick I can find, in case the first method fails.

So it's with a big smile and my seven-foot-tall ex-Sydney bouncer host by my side that I arrive at the front gate of my challenger.

I fancy his wife might have seen *The Parrot* pull up, because as we approach she walks away with a smirk on her face, perhaps noticing the microphone and anticipating what's coming.

At that point my challenger steps out from behind a shed and sizes us up. He isn't a big man, but a fit-looking fifty and country lean, and he, too, is wielding a half-grin.

'G'day,' I say 'I'm the bloke you had a tilt at this morning. And I was just wondering if you wouldn't mind having a chat with me about the status of the road.'

As it happens he doesn't mind at all, and before long he and his wife have us sat down with a cup of tea, ready to answer my questions. I start with the obvious.

'Oh, well, we're just not used to people walking up and down the roads,' he answers. 'You know, we don't know what you're doing and where you come from. You gave my wife a shock.'

'But it is a public road, isn't it?'

'No, only to a certain degree. The council don't maintain the road, and we're expected to cover it for insurance. We've got to have public liability.'

'So if I fell over and broke my leg you'd have to cover me?'

'Well it's a pretty grey area. Some authorities say we've got to cover you, but we say we don't.'

'What about if you'd sooled the dogs onto me, like you threatened?'

'We can't control our dogs,' he says with a big laugh, 'if someone's sneakin' around the joint.'

'So you're a fan of having dogs around?'

'Yeah, they're good because they let you know what's goin' on. As long as they stay in their own yards. When we first came here nearly thirty years ago we had horses, and some of the local dogs used to get in and chase the mares when they were foaling to get the afterbirth. So we told the neighbours we were about to start shooting them, and they told us to go ahead because their dogs shouldn't be there in the first place.'

'You haven't still got that bloody weapon have you?'

'No, they took it off me.'

And there are more laughs. In fact, the whole interview, which started off on shaky ground, has turned amusing. Like the tension has found a release valve we're all happy to pull.

'So am I right in saying you don't see a lot of passing traffic here?'

'None, if we can help it. We get people sometimes who start at the other end of the road, and there's five gates you've got to open, and they get themselves lost and leave the gates open and cattle go everywhere.'

'My understanding is you're entitled to put up a "Private Property, Please Close the Gate" sign, but beyond that you can't stop the traffic. Is that right?'

'No, we can lock the gates, as long as we tell the relevant authorities where the key is. But the dogs are free to come and go as they please,' he says with a smile.

'We've just lost a few dogs, actually. To baits, I think.'

'Who's setting baits?'

'Don't know. They set 'em for the wild dogs.'

'Maybe it was pedestrians trying to clear the path.'

'I doubt it. They don't normally get up this far. We chain the dogs to that wire run out there, so they can dash out and have a go at anyone goin' past.'

'They make movies out of people like you, you know.'

'*Deliverance*? Yeah, I know,' he says, laughing again. 'We just like to qualify people.'

'Then they get a cup of tea,' I say.

'If they're lucky,' he says. 'And if they're real lucky they might even get a biscuit.'

'So how come I got this far up the road, anyway?'

'Our good watchdog just got run over,' he tells me. 'And I told you we lost the others. So we're waitin' on some dogs right now.'

So the bastard was firing blanks all along. And we didn't get a biscuit, either.

LIFE MATTERS

Sometimes the word irrepressible is not enough. Sometimes it just doesn't convey the amount of life in a thing.

A little girl with red hair and an impish smile teaches me that. It's her first day of school and I ask what she's going to do when she gets there.

'Learn and listen,' she says in a voice that could stop a war.

'And do you think you can do that?'

'Yes,' she replies, with a slight lisp.

I'm talking to her mum and dad as well, but she knows it's all about her, and when she talks into the microphone she holds it tightly in both hands, letting go with one hand only to push her younger sister away while she holds court.

'Did you ever think you'd see the day you'd be sending her off to school?' I ask her mother.

'Well, I remember back to when she was first born,' she begins, 'before she even had surgery, so the very first week. And I remember looking at this tiny little five-pound baby, and I had tears rolling down my cheeks, and I thought, "She's never going to get to do any of the firsts: she's never going to ride a bike, she's never going to ride a horse, she's never going to go to school, or learn to read and write, she's never going to get to do any of those things you want for your child when you first see them born."'

'How do you think she'll go at school?'

'I think she'll go well. I don't know how the teachers are going to cope,' she says, through laughter.

'No seriously,' she continues, 'I think she'll go really well. She's a really bright, vibrant little kid.'

'So why was it doubtful that she'd reach school age?'

'When my wife was twenty weeks pregnant,' says the husband, 'we were told the baby wouldn't live because she had a very serious heart condition called hypoplastic left-heart syndrome – it's where the left side of the heart doesn't form, so she only has a right atrium and a right ventricle.

'As you can imagine, we didn't hold much hope. But we got on the internet and did a search on hypoplastic left-heart syndrome, and up came the name of a surgeon in the States who was doing some experimental surgery on kids with this condition.

'So I called and his secretary put me straight through to the doctor, and he said he couldn't promise anything but if we got over there he'd do his best.

'So we sold everything we owned and moved to America.'

He's a bear of a man with short fair hair and a gentle face, and she's small and dark with striking good looks and olive skin.

'I was twenty-nine weeks when we went over,' she continues the story, 'and I carried her till I was thirty-six weeks when I had to have an emergency caesarean section because she had the umbilical cord wrapped around her neck, in addition to her heart problem, so she was basically dead when she was born.

'Then she had her first surgery when she was a couple of weeks old. Basically what they did was put bands around her pulmonary arteries and a stent in the patent ductus arteriosis – the hole in her heart – to keep it open.'

'What followed that one?'

'The experimental surgery was done when she was six months old – she was a little bit bigger, and stronger, and she was more able to cope – and what they did then was repair her circulation. They didn't actually make her a new half a heart, what they did was reconstruct the way the blood actually flows around her body.'

'So how does it flow now?'

'It's a one-way circulation, and now after her third surgery – which happened when she was almost three – she now has a Fontan circulation, which is a one-way passive blood flow around the body.'

'The way it works is the blood passes from the right atrium to the right ventricle,' the husband explains, 'which pumps it through to the body via the aorta and the rest of the circulatory system, then it returns passively to the lungs through siphon and vacuum, before it's gravity-fed back to the heart to start the process over.'

Talking to this couple is almost like talking to one very well informed person. They give each other space, and time, and add value to each other's points when they speak. It's the classic survivor routine, and the balance of power is just right.

'Were you ever advised to terminate?'

'Actually I was advised to terminate straight away,' she says. 'When I had the ultrasound at twenty weeks, the gynaecologist took us into his room and said, "You're baby's not going to survive after it's born, so you should terminate now." And he actually booked us in for a termination the next day.

'But my husband and I had already discussed, when we were planning on having children, that we'd take whatever we got and love them regardless.'

And right on cue the gaggle of girls they've now got erupt in a squealdom of noise. The two adults and three kids are living in a two-room converted garage on their country block while they build their family home. Because it's been raining, the kids have been raising tadpoles inside, and when a frog escapes it's squeals all round.

'I actually had one lady approach us when we were in the street fundraising,' she continues, 'and she told me I was doing the wrong thing and I should let my baby die, because it was obviously God's will that she should die.

'And I just very kindly told her that God gave us a brain, and with that brain we should be able to make decisions, and if those decisions lead to us saving our child then that would be God's will also.

'But that's really rare. For the most part people are really pleased to see the beautiful, crazy little girl who's running around today.'

'Have you had a lot of support from the public?'

'We have,' the husband says. 'We've raised about $170,000 in donations, which really helps, because the hospital was kind enough to carry our debt, providing we don't miss a payment, so that's like a Godsend to us.

'And none of the donations are from millionaires. They're from families with three kids of their own, paying off mortgages on their homes, you know? One donation that springs to mind was from Peter and Pat, that's all it said on the bank statement: Lots of love, Peter and Pat. And they gave us $2000. And we've no idea who they are. Most of the people who give don't want recognition, they just do it because they love people, and they love life.'

'And what do you think about all this?' I ask the little girl of the moment.

'I'm excited to go to big school when I'm already five,' she says, grabbing the microphone.

'And what are you going to take for lunch?'

'Maybe my olives, and my fetta cheese.'

'Have you got any friends at school you already know?'

'Yes, Marlene, Mahalia …'

'That's your big sister.'

'I know,' she says in a way that makes me realise what a dumb thing I said.

'And will she look after you?'

'We look after each other,' she says, earnestly. 'She looks after me, and I look after her.'

GREENHORN FARMING

One fine morning when the world was smiling I watched a man mustering cattle with a four-wheel-drive ute. At first it wasn't clear what he was up to and I thought he was simply driving across the paddock to reach them. But when he flanked the perimeter of the mob and started tooting his horn I realised I was witnessing something special.

The cattle responded by moving around a bit in no particular direction, so his next manoeuvre was to drive through the middle of the herd, still beeping away on the Land Rover's tinny little horn. The beasts calmly stepped aside to allow him passage, before resuming whatever bovine things they were doing before he arrived.

Then he turned and rounded them again, this time managing to get them started in a direction he was happy with. Unfortunately, once he'd driven past each beast it stopped moving and his utility looked like being the only thing in the paddock likely to go through the open gate. The cattle were spread out far and wide behind him, grazing unconcernedly.

The exercise was all performed at about five kilometres an hour, and from my vantage point on the hill overlooking his paddock it made for an amusing spectacle.

Later I meet the man and ask him about his iron horse mustering. He just laughs and tells me I should have seen him trying to do it with his two-wheel-drive vehicle, which he couldn't even steer in the wet grass.

'Have you never heard of a dog?' I ask him.

'Well, I read somewhere that the best cattle dog is one you can take fishing with you,' he explained, 'and since I always take the ute …'

He's a man in his mid-forties with a lean build and a cheeky face that always looks balanced on the verge between grinning and laughing. For over twenty years he was a chef on the Gold Coast, before deciding to change tack and become a cattle farmer.

'Just like that,' he says, with a click of his thumb and forefinger. 'At the blink of an eye, I thought, "Yeah I'll go to the country and buy a little bit of land and run some cattle."'

'Why did you pick here?'

'I like the area. And I like the township: it's just the right size. Oh, and the parking,' he remembers. 'That's the main thing. You can always find a park in town where you can open your door and not hit the car next to you. And there's no parking meters.'

We both laugh at the absurdity.

'How many head of cattle have you got?'

'I bought thirty head.'

'Has it been a steep learning curve?'

'Very,' he says. 'For the first six months I was over at the neighbour's every week saying, "What's wrong with my cattle this time? Why are yours so healthy and mine are always getting sick?"'

And he tells me a story about dehorning, and how the holes left after the horns are sculpted from the beast's skull are left for the flies to blow so the maggots can clean up the wound; a fact he didn't know until one of his previously dehorned heifers started thrashing her head around in the yard and sprayed him with maggots.

And I can only imagine the delight his neighbour would have felt hearing that one.

'What breed are you running?' I ask

'Charolais–Santa Gerudis cross,' he tells me.

'You mean Santa Gertrudis,' I correct him.

'Is it?' he asks, genuinely unsure, but not surprised he got it wrong.

At this point in the interview we're both laughing hard, and for the next hour or so he entertains me with his city-turned-country-bumpkin tales.

'Well, whatever they're called, you just don't know what you're getting,' he says, about the breed of the cattle. 'So you've just got to take the word of the farmer.

'And they can see me coming a mile off.' And he laughs again.

'Like that cattle yard down there. Did you see that thing? All I did was casually mention to one of the cockies that I probably needed to have a yard built at some stage, and the next thing I've got myself the Taj Mahal of cattle yards and I owe him a fortune. All I'd have to do is line and clad the thing and I could live in it!'

'And those Herefords there in my bottom paddock? They're not mine: they're another neighbour's. As soon as he knew I had a good bull he moved his cattle into the paddock next door because he knew they'd climb through the fence to get to my bull, or the other way round.

'In the end I thought it better to let them in because I didn't want my bull getting himself caught up trying to get to them. I've heard of bulls ending up with bent dicks trying to get at cows through fences, and then they're no good for anything but mince. But now I've not only got them all pregnant for him, but I'm feeding them as well.'

'What's you're bull?'

'He's a Murray Grey. We call him Muzza.'

'Have you got names for all your cows?'

'Of course. We've got Cowabunga, Hugh Heifer, Billy Idol with the cute fringe, and we've got one really small one we call Minogue.'

'Are you making enough out of the cattle to survive?'

'No, definitely not.'

'Are you having to pick up other work?'

'Terrible, yes,' he says, with a self-derisive laugh. 'Terrible work. Terrible hours. Terrible pay. Brickies' labouring. My hands'll never be the same.'

'But you're enjoying yourself otherwise?'

'Yeah, it's great. I'm enjoying being in the country without the stress of The Coast. And learning about cattle.'

'I'll tell you one thing I learned about cattle, myself, recently,' I say. 'A bloke told me they fill themselves with air so they can negotiate floodwaters.'

'Yeah, they do,' my greenhorn farmer assures me. 'Air and water. Because if they have too much air they'll be forever tipping over, so they take on water to stabilise.'

'So you're trying to tell me they take on ballast?'

'They take on ballast and air so they can ride the rapids,' he tells me, straight-faced for the first time since we started talking. 'It's only when they get hooked up in fences or logs that they drown.'

'I swear if I stay in this area any longer,' I say, 'you'll all have me believing pigs fly!'

'It's true,' he says, laughing his head off again. 'I've seen them do it.'

COTTON TALES

I'm on the water trail. Just for the exercise I thought I'd retrace some of last year's route to see how the rain has changed fortunes.

The Condamine–Balonne is a mighty river system servicing a fertile belt of land from the Darling Downs in south-east Queensland, to almost as far west as Roma to the north, and just beyond St George to the south. Then the system crosses into New South Wales to join the Darling.

Driving through this catchment area six months ago the whole region was bone dry, and what land was being cropped was mostly under cotton. This time around it's lovely and green with acres of rusty brown sorghum heads ready to be harvested. I ask one farmer why the switch from cotton.

'Mainly because of the water aspect,' he tells me. 'There was no water in any of the dams at the time, and sorghum had jumped up in price while cotton had gone down about a hundred dollars a bale. And for the small amount of cotton I could grow with the allocation I had, dollar for dollar the return was just as good with sorghum.'

The main reason sorghum has jumped in price is the worldwide demand for ethanol has increased, and sorghum is a favoured raw material in its production.

Another farmer in the region took a risk on cotton.

'We took the punt and gambled on late summer rainfall, which we ended up getting,' he tells me.

Farming talk is often peppered with terms used at the racetrack, and the favourite is always water.

That same grower has also been involved in the drafting of a water plan for the Condamine–Balonne catchment, which he expects the Queensland government to sign off on by the middle of the year.

'How's the relationship between irrigators on this side of the border and your counterparts in New South Wales?' I ask him.

'Well, that's always a sticky one, and I guess there is a fair bit of controversy in the lower Balonne. All we do on this side is take the peaks out of the flow. And with this plan not everyone gets what they want – and that includes our farmers – but what we've got is an acceptable outcome for the whole community.'

I wonder which community he means.

As I head west it's a joy to see so much water; every crossing seems to be through or over a swollen, swirling brown river, every weir is overflowing, every dam is full.

Along the way, the name Cubbie Station keeps cropping up. I'm sure you've heard the story: a cotton property large enough to be seen from space uses bulldozers to divert the Culgoa River into storage dams with the holding capacity of Sydney Harbour, all without an environmental impact study and with approval from the Queensland government.

Naturally I want to talk to the Cubbie operators, so I set myself up in nearby Dirranbandi and put a bid in for an interview. While I wait for a response I talk to a few locals.

One local of seventy-five years reckons the two biggest changes he's seen in the area are cotton and Buffel Grass, the local cattle farmers' favourite pasture improver, which is also making a pest of itself with its monoculture tendencies. I ask about Cubbie.

'I'd say it's been good for this town, Cubbie,' he says to me. 'Employs a lot of people. And people who complain about it don't know the facts and figures, simple as that.'

'People downstream in New South Wales say their floodplains don't see the flooding they used to because of Cubbie; do you think there's any truth in that?'

'No, I don't,' he answers, unequivocally. 'Anything Cubbie's done they've been licensed for. And people downstream don't know what they're talking about, because when they put in Beardmore Dam that took away a lot of the small floods.'

Beardmore Dam, completed in 1972 specifically for the St George area's irrigation needs, holds less than 100,000 megalitres; well under a quarter of Cubbie's capacity.

Another local tells me I wouldn't find a more water-conscious operation anywhere in the world, no less.

'The manager is very conscious of every litre of water used,' she tells me. 'And anyone with any concerns is encouraged to go out and have a look for themselves. I'm sure he'll welcome you with open arms and you'll be very impressed after you've spoken to him.'

Unfortunately the manager wouldn't speak to me – perhaps I wasn't worthy, or perhaps he just didn't want me to see how much water was running into his dams – and I left unenlightened and unimpressed.

I carry on downstream to a riverfront property on the floodplains south of the border, and the contrast between the system above and below the border is staggering. There the Culgoa (as the main stream becomes in New South Wales) is no longer a river in flood, but just a river running at about half-bank level.

It looks like someone's pulled the plug out.

The managers of that property tell me they have records dating back over a hundred years that show the waterhole at the homestead only drying up twice in that time; both occurrences in the past ten years, since the heavy irrigation began upstream.

I track down a cotton industry heavyweight and tell him what I've seen.

'Certainly there are some extractions going because there has been a flood,' he tells me. 'But we really need to be looking at the long-term flows, the long-term extractions, and let the science make some of the decisions. You just can't go out there and have a look on one day; I think sometimes that can be misleading.'

'But so can statistics.'

'Yeah, that's right,' he agrees, with professional courtesy, 'and that's why we need a full debate.'

'Do you think the amount of water Cubbie Station is taking out of the system is ethical?' I ask him.

'Look, they're really efficient users of the resource,' he defends. 'They've done an enormous amount of work to limit evaporation by deepening their storage facilities, they're using state-of-the-art scheduling techniques, so they're using the resource to the best of their ability and generating income.'

'But to some degree at the expense of people downstream.'

'Look, that's the debate that the industry has to have.'

I loved the snippet about Cubbie limiting its evaporation

problem by deepening its storage facilities. We should all be grateful for their thoughtfulness.

Another grazier on the floodplains south of Cubbie tells me it's really just a transfer of wealth from downstream to upstream, and the reduced flows are exactly what they expected.

'The Queensland Department of Natural Resources submitted figures to a 2002 government report on the impact of development in the Lower Balonne,' he tells me, 'which didn't pull any punches. Their summation was that small floods would disappear, medium floods would become small floods, and major floods would be severely impacted, and that's exactly what is happening.

'The point is,' he continues, 'it's the level of extraction the Queensland government has allowed to take place. There is room for irrigation on these systems, but not to the level that has been allowed.'

'But irrigators stockpiling water upstream,' I say, 'to the detriment of those downstream isn't exclusive to Queensland. It's happened in New South Wales, and Victoria, and South Australians probably dream about doing it.'

'No, and you're quite correct,' the grazier agrees, 'the problems on the floodplains of the Lower Lachlan, the Lower Murrumbidgee, they've been becoming "desertified" for a very long time, even longer than up here.

'But I think the sad thing is people don't seem to learn from history.'

So it seems to me the problem isn't cotton. Cotton farmers are irrigators first and foremost, and will use their allocation growing whatever they think will give them the best return. Furthermore and contrary to popular belief, cotton is by no means the thirstiest summer crop – at least according to Cotton Australia's figures – rating better than tomatoes and corn, for instance, and a long way more efficient than rice and lucerne hay.

The real problem is a mismanagement of the resource at a state government level. Some river systems are simply over-allocated, and when the system's in flood you don't need a CSIRO report to see it.

KIDDING AROUND

It's true what they say about goats: they're horny bastards. Or at least the billies are. I'm not sure the nannies are so enthusiastic about it all.

I'm on a quad bike looking for goats with a farmer who's been successfully farming feral goats on a property on the Culgoa floodplains. It's mainly lignum and coolibah country with some dogwood for variety, and the goats aren't as easy to locate as they were before the rain.

When we finally do see a mob it's already making away from us in the semi-dense scrub, and I'm not sure my eyes are telling me the truth.

'Is it possible I just saw one of those billies trying to mount a nanny while they were running away?' I ask my host when I pull up beside him.

'More than probably,' he says. 'They're not too fussy where or when or how.'

'But they've also got to be pretty agile to pull that stunt off.'

'I'm not too sure they're all that successful on the run, but they keep trying till they get a win.'

He gives the dog a command and it jumps from the back of his bike and sets to work bringing the mob back to us.

'The billies are very hard on the females when they're mating,' he says. 'If she lies down they'll dig their horns in under her and make her stand up so they can do the business,' he says. 'I had my father up recently and he couldn't bear to watch, they're so cruel.'

There are about a hundred and fifty goats of every colour, shape and size you can imagine. The dog has brought them in to about twenty metres and I fancy you can see every breed of goat that ever was manifest in the mob before us.

'About the only colour I've never seen is green,' the farmer tells me.

In truth they are mostly coloured brown, black and white, with Cashmere and Angora the dominant strains, since they were the main breeds brought out by the first European settlers. Attempts have been made to introduce Boer into the gene pool to increase bulk, with limited success. But it's a motley sight, nonetheless, against the muted greens of the Australian scrub.

'Those little ones there, probably no more than ten, fifteen kilos' he says, pointing out three goats about the same size as the cattle dog, 'they would be in kid; they'd have had the job done on them already.

'They can kid twice a year if things are right, and they often throw twins and triplets. So a mob can double in size every year if it's not controlled.'

We move on through the rejuvenated country and the smell of a thousand grasses in flower makes me smile. Zebra and Chestnut Finches explode from the tufts in front of the bikes and every so often we startle a kangaroo or a pig. The sky is innocent blue and the clouds are doing their cotton thing.

The farmer points out the grazing line of the goats at about the one-and-a-half-metre mark, or as high as the billies can reach standing on their hind legs. It's as level as a laser line. Goats don't graze at ground level but feed on the leaves of bushes and trees, and they can be devastating on the native vegetation.

'It's really only been in the last fifteen years or so the industry got organised enough to be an effective control on numbers,' he tells me. 'Before that it was more an opportunistic thing; where the local footy club would have a weekend away mustering a couple of hundred goats, which they'd sell to the abattoirs for pet food.

'But then a couple of the abattoirs started specialising in goats and opened up markets offshore – the Hispanic community in America's a big customer of ours, Indonesia, Germany – it's the most commonly eaten meat in the world.'

'Do you eat them?'

'Yeah, when they're small enough. Taste just like lamb.'

He shows me their mustering yards and the electrified fencing at ground level so the goats don't climb under it, and his trapping system, which is no more than a couple of logs leaning against a fence allowing access into a paddock with a water trough.

'The simpler the better. They'll climb up anything, and they need to drink, so we just let them come and go for a few days and then remove their escape route.

'They're a lot smarter than sheep,' he tells me. 'Put a sheep dog onto goats for the first time and they don't know what to make of them. Goat goes up a tree and the dog looks back at you as if to say, "What do we do now boss? This one climbs trees!"'

Listening to him talk about the goats you'd think he's been working them all of his forty or so years, but in fact he was a plumber on the coast up until eighteen months ago. One day he said to his wife, 'This is killing me; let's go bush.' So they applied for the management rights to this station and surprised themselves by getting the job. Now they're both happier with life.

We find another mob, a bigger mob this time, and he points out some large billies.

'It's a good thing we're upwind of those boys or you'd be able to smell them from here. They get a fair old stink up at times, especially when they're rutting. They piddle all over themselves and everything else while they're at it.

'But the mob tends to be run by the nannies. The billies only join the mob to get among the girls. Most of the time they run together with the other billies.'

'So they hang out with the boys till it's time to come in and make a nuisance of themselves with the girls, smelling of stale piss. Where have I heard that before?'

'And then they start fighting each other, too. Just like the pub.'

KAMIKAZE CARP

The strangest thing I came across driving through the floods was carp jumping onto the roadside to die in the sun.

It was in Moonie River country and I'd just taken *The Parrot* through a few deepwater crossings – about half a metre – when I came across a man shovelling topsoil from a box trailer onto what looked to be a pile of fish. So I stopped.

Sure enough there are twenty or thirty large carp in a loose heap that he is covering with dirt. Most of the fish are days dead and decidedly on the nose, and he is trying to bury them so they won't assault the olfactory senses of passers-by.

There is no sign of water across the road where the fish are, but there's a culvert straddling a bulging brown stream below. Somehow the fish have managed to get from the water up onto the road.

'What they're doin' is they're swimmin' against the current,' the man on the shovel tells me, 'and once they get to the wall they jump.'

He is a stocky man with dark skin and a big, broad grin. Sweat marks are just beginning to show on the chest and under the arms of his blue singlet, and neither of us can take our eyes off the sight before us.

'Was there water across the road when they jumped?'

'Not where we're standing,' he says. 'They just jumped clean over that wall up onto the road.'

'They're big fish. Some of them would be twenty kilos, surely.'

'Well that big one there would be, easy,' he agrees, nodding towards the biggest of them.

'Have you seen this before?'

'No, first time I've ever seen it,' he shakes his head.

'I've seen them left high and dry when the waters go down, but I've never seen them jump to their death before.'

'Well, they were probably jumping about a foot and a half to get up over the wall.'

'Just to die in the sun,' I state the obvious. 'There's something really stupid about that plan.'

Among the dead there are also a few hundred fingerlings flapping away like silver tinsel in the breeze. He tells me he caught those in his yabby pots while he was watching the fish jump the wall, before he got sick of pulling them out of his pots and gave up on the yabby fishing.

'The shopkeeper was the first to see the carp,' he says. 'He was just walking along here and he saw one jump out in front of him. And we didn't know whether to believe him or not, so we came out and sat around watching; next minute one went over, then another one.'

'Why are they coming upstream?'

'I think it's just instinct.'

'Surely not to breed. From what I know of carp they breed anywhere.'

'Yeah, I think they breed out there,' he says, indicating back downstream. 'But this is the first really big flush this system has had for a while, and they're just following the run of the water now.'

'I always knew they were stupid,' is my scientific observation. 'And now we've got proof. They jump over walls to their death.'

I leave him chuckling and gagging in equal parts – the stench is truly palpable – to continue his Good Samaritan duties, and I drive on, wondering.

The fingerlings I understand. At the moment these outback rivers are teeming with fingerlings of all types, no doubt a natural survival response that kicks in during a flood. Stop at any weir and you'll see thousands of the buggers making their way upstream, or even crossing the road in numbers in two inches of water: the birds think it's Christmas.

But the carp I don't get. Why would they leap from a perfectly good river to a fate unknown?

The next day I run into some girls working for South West Natural Resource Management who have the answer.

'I actually live on the Paroo,' begins one of the girls, 'which is one of the few river systems without a big carp problem, because it only flows into the Darling in very wet years.

'But they are very vigorous in their colonisation techniques, so if they come across any kind of obstacle that stops them from getting upstream – like a log or a build-up of debris – their natural instinct is to jump it.

'So, when they come up against an obstacle like a weir or a culvert, they can still feel the flow of the river through the pipes so they try to jump it, thinking it's a log or a small obstacle, and end up flapping about on dry land.'

'It's a behaviour pattern that's taken advantage of,' says the other girl, 'to make effective carp traps in conjunction with fish ladders. And it works on the principle that native fish will continually swim around barriers, so they'll move through a fish passage system, whereas a carp will jump as soon as it gets to the first obstacle in its way.'

'So it's like a holding bay beyond the first obstacle?'

'Basically, yes, to remove carp from the waterway.'

'Have either of you ever seen this stunt?'

'Yes, I've seen it,' says the first girl. 'I guess it is an odd thing, but we just put it down to the fact that carp are a bit silly.'

'That's what I thought!'

'But they've been so successful infiltrating our native rivers it's obviously a very effective strategy.'

Jump to conquer. Or die.

MY DARLING

I spent a night listening to the Darling River run. I camped at Nineteen Mile weir, just outside Bourke, and sat before the fire and listened. A three-quarter moon was shining on the surface and highlighting the flow, and the water pouring over the weir sounded good.

Earlier I'd caught some shrimp in an old twenty-litre tin with holes in the bottom – obviously fashioned for the purpose – using a rotting carp I found on the bank as bait. Then I sat in a deckchair and caught Yellowbelly; none big enough to keep for eating, though each one a little joy to catch. People in town told me big fish were being caught, but it was all the same to me.

A stand of old river gums shaded me from the afternoon sun and cautious Budgerigars skittered down a dead limb in the water to drink. In the background I could hear Linnets and Brown Treecreepers, and always the flow of the river, always the flow.

The water wasn't quite the milky-tea colour people speak of; more like slightly opaque milk coffee with a greenish tinge I'd be highly suspicious of in a cup of tea. Flotillas of water spiders skipped upstream while a gentle breeze rippled the surface. There was green pick along the banks.

As night fell I spread the fire and pan-fried a steak on the coals – excellent eye fillet from Dirranbandi – which I ate with steamed vegetables and a bottle of red wine. Then I went to bed as contented as any man, and let the river lull me to sleep.

Sometimes I think I'm going feral. I've always been happy with my own company; lately I've been feeling like I'm no longer suited to polite society.

I used to seek out the company of men; now I think I get my fill of them in the course of doing my work. By day's end I'm happy to walk away. We don't need each other to survive.

I also used to crave the attentions of women; now I think I've grown out of them. I feel like I've graduated from the School of Testosterone – I wouldn't say with honours, but certainly with enthusiasm – and now I'm free.

Of course all this might be nothing more serious than libido's appropriate response to drought, and all it will take is one false move to reignite that wretched flame of indecency every man knows lives within him; but for now I am calm, and happy to be left alone. I've even got the show on a need-to-know basis with regards to my whereabouts: if Charlie asks where I am, I tell him I'm at large. The nearest they get to knowing my whereabouts is by the location of my stories, which I don't always file in order. I'm getting more like Colonel Kurtz in *Apocalypse Now* every day.

I do think about you all, though.

I think about my daughter and how she is facing the future, and my father and how he is nearing the end. I have imagined burying him, but I cannot allow myself to imagine the same of my daughter. Sometimes I horrify myself by thinking of harm coming to her and I must forcibly remove the thought from my head, it shakes me so. A week back I saw a large brown snake on the road, dead in the act of trying to swallow a spiny lizard of some sort, and I shuddered as I imagined Benino being bitten by a snake, then agonised for an hour trying to remember the treatment of choice for snakebite these days.*

I also think about the lessons some of you offered before I was ready to learn them, and shake my head in wonder at some of the truly stupid things I've done. And I think about the few pearls of wisdom I've managed to scrape together – a couple by design, most by accident, together, I fear, not enough to make a bracelet for a child to wear – and try to imagine who might want them.

And I think of people I have met along the way who have made an impact, good and bad, and wonder how they are these days. Mostly I wish them well. And by that I don't mean most of them I wish well, and some I don't; rather, most of the time I am big enough to wish them all well, and only on rare occasions does mean-spiritedness fill me with such devilish joy that I would have the bastards dead at my own hands.

I met an eighty-four-year-old woman yesterday who was managing a pub single-handed, and I asked her what she'd learned about people serving behind a bar.

'That there's lovely, good things in most people,' she answered without hesitation, making me wonder if she ever has murderous thoughts. She doesn't drink or smoke and refuses to have poker machines in the place because, she says, 'There's something in my conscience that won't allow me to put poker machines in front of people who have a problem.'

But even a saint casts a shadow, and she admits to loving the horses and being a regular Saturday morning punter. Before she dies she wants to fly down to Melbourne for Derby Day and see the horses go round again.

She looks like Spike Milligan and tells me she's proud of Australia. I ask her why.

'The beautiful country we live in. I love the peace. This western country; I love the contrasts between the red soil and the green, the beautiful trees, and the birds.'

'Are we going to bury you out the back?'

'Oh, yes,' she says with genuine enthusiasm, 'out with the cattle and the sheep and the birds, underneath a coolibah tree, in a wool bale.'

Earlier in the day I'd met another lovely soul. He was a sheep grazier who just happened to have a small opal-mining town spring up along a bore drain on his property. He tells me he didn't mind until it had grown to about a hundred residents and it was brought to his attention that he was responsible for the whole settlement.

'Yeah, we all got on pretty well together,' he says, as if he's talking about a gathering no larger than a couple of mates in the pub. 'And they wanted an airstrip so I said, 'Yeah, have a loan of the tractor; build yourselves an airstrip.'

'Anyway it gets to the stage where the flying doctor starts to visit and one day I got talking to the pilot, who asked me whose airstrip it was. So I told him the miners put it in but it was on my property, and he said, 'You'd be responsible for this. If a plane goes down you'll be out here digging a hole.'

'So I looked into it, and found out not only was I responsible for the airstrip but I was responsible for all the houses and everything else,' he says, laughing at the memory.

'Anyway, I panicked a bit, and jumped in the car and drove to Brisbane, and sold seven hundred acres and the bore to the government, who then presented it to the local shire council and they took the responsibility.'

And he's such an easy-going, likeable man you can well imagine how an entire community of a hundred or so people could develop in his front yard without it bothering him. He tells me a few stories about life as the accidental governor, but none more memorable than this:

'At this stage of the game I was a bachelor,' he begins, 'and there was this woman with three little children turns up in the bottom paddock and sets up camp illegally, outside the main area.

'So I went to see the mining warden and he agreed that she had to move, but he was frightened to tell her because he'd already had a fair old fight with her over it. And I couldn't get her to move. So in the end I thought I'd better try a civilised approach and invite her up to the house for tea.

'Anyway, that was thirty years ago,' he says. 'And she still hasn't left. She just upgraded her accommodation from the paddock to the house.'

It's a sweet story he's no doubt told many times, but his eyes sparkle when he delivers the punchline and you know he'd do it exactly the same way next time around.

When I leave he bids me safe travels, and warns me to watch out for illegal campers. I tell him I will, but sitting out here in the firelight listening to the river pulse I can't see any sort of camper any place near.

* I decided on no tourniquet, immobilise affected limb, keep patient quiet, and drive like a banshee.

THE FOXACENE

Deep in the jungles of northern New South Wales I almost became a household name for introducing the world to an animal so rare even it didn't know what it was.

It all started one hot afternoon when I was enjoying a few beers in The Parrot Bar in the Van Park Hotel at Whereverthehelliwas, and I decided to ring a mate of mine to enjoy some of his decidedly unique humour and wit. And it was in the course of that amusing conversation that he told me of the never-before-sighted creature that apparently washed up out of the floods in northern New South Wales, and had taken to visiting my mate's sister's house.

'She reckons it looks like a cross between a fox and a kangaroo,' he told me, 'and it's been coming up to eat the dog biscuits and play with the family pet. They've never seen anything like it, and nor has anyone else in town.'

So he gave me his sister's number and I duly rang her, but she was not impressed.

'We've decided to manage it from this end, thank you,' was the polite response I got when I started asking about the creature. 'But we'll call you if we change our mind and decide to talk.'

Now there is nothing in the world that piques the interest of the media more than that sort of response. Where I was only half-keen when I first heard the story – the location being a full day's drive from where I was at the time – now my mind was racing with thoughts of a new discovery in the animal kingdom. Indeed, had I not already been well beyond the legal blood-alcohol limit for driving a motor vehicle I would have set off immediately.

Instead I wait till the following day, and by afternoon find myself driving into the small village nominated by my mate as the one inhabited by his sister. Under the circumstances I had already determined stealth would be my best friend on this assignment, so I creep through the town as surreptitiously as one can in a six-by-three-metre travelling advertisement, and find a park in a quiet street.

I barely walk twenty metres before I'm recognised by a local sitting on his porch – first, mistakenly, as the host of the show whose portrait adorns the van; then, loudly, as my own incognito self – and invited in for a beer.

Cover blown I figure I might as well be upfront, and I ask my new best friend if he knows anything about the strange animal seen hereabouts.

'Well, I'm led to believe,' he begins, 'that on one particular evening there was a bit of a commotion on the back verandah of one of the local's houses, and after investigation a creature was found at the dog's bowl eating the dog's biscuits.

'Now you'd think any animal coming up and having a go at the dog's tucker would be fairly tame, but the people who witnessed it maintain it's an unknown creature.'

'Can you describe it for me?'

'Well I was told it had a fox-like face, rather large hind legs in comparison to the front legs, and a very long tail. Not a bushy tail, but a long kangaroo-like tail.'

'Could it be, perhaps, a cross between a kangaroo and a dog?'

'At a fair stretch,' he says, laughing, 'I suppose you could say that after a long session at the public house at the bottom of the street.'

'I've also heard it has an unusual gait.'

'No, I haven't heard that one. But a lot of people in this area have an unusual gait,' he confirms, 'at certain times of the day.'

Then he points me in the direction of another local who had seen the creature and we bid farewell.

Now it just so happens that as I approach the front door of this other witness's home I overhear the following conversation:

'… and then I told him, "No thanks, we don't need any radio reporters around here. We're looking after it ourselves from here on in," and sent the poor bugger on his way.'

So naturally when I reach the flyscreen door I introduce myself thus:

'Good afternoon. My name is Monte Dwyer, and I presume I'm the poor bugger you're referring to.'

At the dining table just inside the door sit three people, all of whom turn towards me and say absolutely nothing. The closest to me is a man with a beard who looks like he's just knocked off work. He's frozen in the act of rolling a cigarette. At the far end of the table is a woman – presumably the other witness I'd been sent to see – who has a beer poised between the table and her mouth so I can't tell which way it's going. And the third, by dint of a strong family resemblance and the fact that she's the last speaker, is obviously the sister of my mate. She looks the most stunned.

She's also the first to regain composure and invite me in for a beer, and during the course of the following discussion about the creature and its recent movements it's determined that I can stay, maybe; pending the reaction of her partner, who is known for his forthright and sometimes gruff manner, and who also happens to be a member of a well-known bikers' gang I have no desire to tangle with. I am on trial.

So she invites me to park *The Parrot* in her backyard, but not plug into mains power lest it be seen as presumptuous, and we saunter up to the public house at the bottom of the street to meet my judge and possible executioner.

Contrary to the stereotypical bikers' image I'd concocted in my mind he is a small man with a reserved dignity, who makes no attempt to include me in his circle whatsoever. I like his style immediately, but it's clear he isn't going to warm to me so readily.

'I'm not happy,' is apparently what he'd said when told of my arrival.

It's an interesting thing to have your personality under scrutiny, and there's nothing you can do but be yourself, but as unobtrusive a version as you can manage. I offer to shout him beers (but make no fuss when he politely refuses), I join the pub's social club in time for the weekly jackpot (and am grateful not to win), I buy raffle tickets (ditto previous qualifier), and I chat politely to all and sit back in the pack and keep my place.

And somewhere through another night of too many beers we find a common interest in speedway bikes and, even though my interest dates back to when I was still a teenager, I remember just enough to be able to engage with him on the subject. The ice is broken. I can stay and wait on his back verandah for the creature to visit that night.

Problem is, nobody told the creature, and by midnight there is still no sign of it. At one point I do fancy I see a much larger creature in the shadows – perhaps an elephant with a koala nose? – yet nothing resembling the descriptions of the creature. So we all retire; my hosts and their neighbours to their own beds inside, and me to *The Parrot* parked in the backyard, not fifteen metres from the bowl of dog biscuits.

Of course within minutes of putting my head down I hear the crunching of doggy biscuits and the creature is there.

At first glance it looks like a common old fox. It has a red-brown pelt with a whitish underbelly and throat, extending to its muzzle, and a black line drawn from the inside of each eye along the nose almost to its tip.

But the tail is all wrong: it's longer by about half than any fox tail I've ever seen, and has a white tip. In addition it isn't at all bushy, and when he (for it's a young dog, not a bitch) holds it extended it does indeed curve like the tail of a kangaroo.

The Tweed Valley area is famous for sightings of a Thylacine-like creature with strong hind legs, often described as looking like a cross between a dog and a kangaroo, and while I couldn't see any exaggeration of the hind quarters I wonder if this long tail isn't the inspiration for many of these sightings. Is this the first close-quarters sighting of a juvenile foxacene we are experiencing?

I take pictures, and the animal seems unperturbed by my presence or the flash of the camera, or the arrival of the others who've returned to the scene after the fox terrier started barking. Indeed the animal is so absorbed in playing with the foxy that he allows me to approach and kneel beside him and offer my hand for a sniff.

Then the mongrel bites me. Not like a dog bites – out of fear or aggression – more like he is sizing my finger up as potential food. The host tells me it had also had a go at her bare foot in a similar fashion the night before, so obviously it isn't a fussy eater.

And neither is it in a hurry to leave, so after we've had our fill of the sight we leave the two animals to their foxy games and go our separate ways: my hosts and their neighbours back to their respective indoor arrangements, and me back to *The Parrot* to dream the dreams of a man on the eve of a great discovery.

Unfortunately when I put my scientific breakthrough to Charlie, he is sceptical and calls in a wildlife expert, who takes one look at the photo I've sent and reduces my foxacene to nothing more exciting than a juvenile fox in summer pelt. He says the tail appears disproportionately long because the fox hasn't yet grown into his bones, and the fur will fill out as winter approaches.

But in my opinion the experts don't know everything. I've held up many a fox by the tail and this one was long by comparison. Furthermore, he couldn't shed any light on the elephant in the shadows, and an elephant with a koala nose can't be an easy thing to miss in Zoology 101. So how can we trust him to know a fox from a foxacene?

SOCIAL CENTRAL

I went to Condobolin because I'd heard they play music to their cattle while they eat. Al fresco. In the moonlight. And I never knew cows could be such cultured diners.

They were Angus cattle, the maestros were breeding; specifically Angus bulls that were destined to one day have their own herd of cows to breed with. Providing, of course, they rated well enough on the Jap B3 Index (a system used to measure everything from weight gain to scrotum size to determine breeding potential).

So these are pampered beasts; the chosen ones, bred for stud duties. I get that. But are they so precious and highly strung that they can't eat without Mozart?

'No, the cattle are as quiet as any other cattle going into a feedlot,' one of the breeders tells me.

'But last year we had a problem in our drought-lot,' she continues. 'We had a lot of young cattle, five hundred six- or seven-month-old calves in the one spot, and that's always asking for trouble; they can be a bit skittish if feral pigs come in from the hills to feed on the grain, because it's a drought. Kangaroos come in as well, and the birds come in to feed along the trough and the wild cats come in to feed on the birds. There's a lot of action up there at night so with that many calves in the one place it can get a bit scary for them.'

'So who came up with the idea to play them music?'

'Well, I guess that was mine,' he says, 'but in some ways it's nothing new. Dairy farmers have been playing music to their cows for years. Horse trainers play music to their thoroughbreds. And old drovers'll tell you how they sang and whistled to their cattle on still nights just to create a constant noise.'

'It's just a matter of breaking up the still night air, is the key to it. Sometimes it can be very, very quiet, and a sudden noise – like the banging of a drum popping in the shed when the temperature changes – can be very scary to them.'

'So we had a spare stereo,' she picks up the thread, 'which we rigged up on the shed next to the drought-lot, and tuned it to one of the radio stations and started playing them music all the time.'

'So what's their taste in music?'

'We chose a rock station because they're young cattle, teenagers really, so they're not going to want to listen to classical.'

'Yeah, we did try a few stations out,' he adds. 'Talkback didn't work; they got too agitated. And when we had it on the ABC they kept falling asleep. But they seem to like classic rock; keeps them happy.'

'And it keeps them stimulated, which is another concern for stock that spend long periods in a confined space.'

Later on that weekend another farmer supports the theory about stock needing stimulation, and even goes so far as to tell me feedlot farmers often give their cattle a big soccer ball to kick around.

I buy it, because I like the notion of soccer-playing cattle and it sounds so bizarre it's probably true, but I have less success convincing my radio colleagues when I tag my story with that snippet.

The same farmer also tells me a story about catching a car full of poachers. It's a big problem in a lot of country areas, and Condobolin was having a spate of it; mostly pig hunters and weekend warriors trespassing on properties, leaving gates open and stealing fuel and machinery. So they were on guard.

'Then some locals over the way came across some guys spotlighting,' he takes up the story, 'so they approached them and the guys bolted.

'They rang the local copper and gave chase, but these guys weren't stopping for anyone or anything, driving straight through fences and closed gates, farm to farm, road to road, sometimes giving the chasers the slip for a spell, then getting picked up again as soon as they set off again, and the local copper was involved by now and he called in some back-up from another station.'

'So it was a full-scale car chase?'

'Oh yeah, at one stage there were three police cars in the chase, plus the locals. And the police were trying to pull them up but there was no way these guys were pulling up.'

The storyteller is young as farmers go, and speaks in a deep voice that barely conceals his wonder at the gall of the poachers. Regardless of which side he was on, it's clear he can appreciate a good story, and gives his characters fair room to develop.

'So eventually they got chased out onto the main road and I guess they figured it was inevitable they'd be caught out there so they ducked into the mines – this was about dawn by now, and they'd been at it since about ten o'clock – and the police wanted to call off the chase because it was too dangerous, too many tracks and mine shafts, but they weren't sure they'd be any better off dealing with the angry mob of farmers they'd have on their hands if they did call it quits.

'Anyway that decision was made for them when one of our mates took his plane up to have a look around, and he spotted them just over the hill from my house. So he called me on the two-way and my mate and I set off after them in the ute.'

Now, just as an aside, I did meet his mate – a highly amusing beanpole of a man with a face like a sculpted smirk and a walk that defied all rules of ambulation – and together I couldn't imagine a less likely pair of apprehenders than the jolly young farmer and the rubber man.

'So then we had aerial surveillance as well and it was a lot easier to stay in touch and know which way they were turning – the pilot reckoned it looked a lot like the OJ Simpson car chase – but we couldn't do much but follow; if you tried to pull up beside them they'd try to ram you.

'Eventually we had them hemmed in with cops and farmers and they just knew they had nowhere to go so they stopped.

'So we pulled up beside them and my mate said, 'Looks like the fun's over, fellas.' And the young bloke in the back looked over and said, 'It hasn't been fun for quite a while.'

'And then the cops arrived and pulled their guns on them, which frightened the shit out of them, and everybody else, I might add.

'But it was good, yeah; finally we've had a win and now we might get people taking us seriously when we say no poaching.'

He gives me a whistle-stop tour of his property and shows me the scar left by a tornado they had late last year. The tornado's path is clear even a couple of months after the event, with broken and uprooted trees in a hundred-metre-wide strip, extending for several kilometres. And in a paddock in the middle of the timbered country are hundreds of sheep carcasses lying where they fell, obviously caught unawares by the ferocity of the tornado.

'It's the debris that does the damage,' he tells me. 'Most of these sheep were killed by flying sticks through their bodies. There were even two of them skewered together on the one branch.'

Is this nature serving up lamb kebabs to remind us what's in store?

WELCOME BAGGAGE AND HARD TRUTHS

That's my daughter, the baggage. She's not the only baggage I've picked up over the years, but she's certainly the lightest. I picked her up in Sydney, which is where I picked her up in the first place, and indeed for the first time, when she was only minutes old. She's coming with me for the last of the trip to learn about the Murray–Darling Basin, the forthcoming federal election, and whatever other pearls of wisdom I might be able to string together for her.

It was her mother's idea. 'Why don't you take her with you on the road for a month,' she said. 'It'll be a good education for her.' I could have kissed her mother for that, only it would have frightened the daylights out of both of us.

And so teachers were contacted, schoolwork organised, and an additional assignment was set for Benino to report back to her classmates twice a week with a travel update.

'Cool,' said Benino. I agreed, and off we set.

We sing as we travel. Me, because I plan on doing some recording when the trip is done and my voice can use all the work I can give it. Benino, for the sheer pleasure of singing.

At the moment our main accompaniment of choice is Harry Nilsson's *Nilsson Schmilsson*, and my daughter comments on my efforts.

'That didn't sound very nice,' she says, screwing up her nose.

'No way!' I object. 'I sing it better than Harry.'

'But Harry's dead, Dad.'

'That's right. So obviously I'm in better voice than him these days.'

'Maybe not,' she says, and we both laugh.

The first port of call is Kiama, south of Wollongong, famous for its blowhole. With a big sea running the blowhole is capable of shooting a spout of water into the air high enough to knock birds from the sky. Some say they've seen fish flapping on the rocks a full two hundred metres away after the wash hissed back into its hole.

Today the sea is so calm the blowhole is no more than a whoomp-fizz-gurgle, with only a lame splash to show for itself.

But we do see dolphins cavorting in the waves around the headland, which is an exciting thing for a ten-year-old, and still a comfort to her father to know they haven't given up on us yet.

From the coast we make a beeline over the mountains heading for Mount Kosciuszko and ultimately the Upper Murray. It's certainly not the quickest way through the alpine reaches, but it may be the prettiest.

The rolling terrain on each uphill approach is television-commercial perfect; as you climb, the road is canopied by eucalypts so it seems as though you're driving through a tunnel, and through breaks in the vegetation the distant valley floors are shockingly beautiful. At times the way was so surreal I fully expected to see a dragon's lair; a notion not shared, I might add, by my daughter, who thought it looked nothing at all like dragon country.

On some plateau country we see a farmer grubbing out weeds with a small adze, so we stop for a chat. He's sixty-six years old and been farming for nearly forty of those years. He's a fit-looking man though his face is ruddy from the brisk mountain air and the exertion of bending to chip away at the little purple weeds.

'We're plagued by Patterson's Curse in this country,' he tells me. 'I used to use chemicals, but we really don't know where it ends up. Where does it go if not back to our stock through the grass, or into the waterways? So now I do it manually.'

He's got twelve hundred acres and he used to run sheep, with only a handful of cattle, but now he's given away the sheep.

'Used to be 186 million sheep in this country. Now we've got 83 million. Just too hard to make them pay.

'Getting harder for any farmer to make a living now. To give you an example, we sold a cow last week, never had a calf, and got 80 cents per kilo. In 1973 we were getting $1.10. You don't have to be Einstein to work it out.

'Markets are too volatile, diesel costs are up, same with insurance, transport, labour costs for slaughtering the animals…'

'Are the kids coming back onto the land?'

'No. No, you can't educate them and expect them to return to live and work on the farm. No monetary gain.'

'So who's going to do the farming?'

'That,' he says, pausing for a long moment, and exhaling as he continues, 'is a good question. I don't know. The average age of farmers on the land is about, say, fifty-eight to sixty-eight, and there are very few kids coming through.

'We've had a brain drain, as we all know, and a lot of kids are going offshore for better opportunities. Those who don't go to the mines.

'Bob Hawke told us during his term that farmers had to either get really big, or go back to hundred-acre holdings, till we could find a balance where we could feed the country.

'Well that's happening, councils are carving up land down to concessional lots as small as twenty and thirty acres, but I'm not sure we're feeding the country.'

'If you had your time over again would you still choose to be a farmer?' I ask.

He takes another deep breath before answering.

'I'd have to think long and hard about that. My heart says yes, but my head says no.

'If my wife had her way we'd be gone tomorrow. She does the books, she's the one who tells me I'm flogging a dead horse.

'It's the women who bear the brunt.'

Then he weeps unashamedly. And he does so, he tells me once he's regained his composure, because it's hard to face the truth.

MURRAY MADNESS

Benino and I are camped on the banks of the River Murray surrounded by angry people. We've been travelling its length from the source at Lakes Hume and Dartmouth, while I try to get my head around the finer points of water trading, along with issues like the proposed pipeline to carry water from the Murray to the people of Melbourne.

To understand the importance of the Murray–Darling system to our agricultural output all you have to do is travel its length for a couple of thousand kilometres and see all the land it irrigates. Put simply, it's the country's agricultural lifeline.

And the anger I've seen over the past couple of days is very real. People won't talk to me on the record or off, because they're afraid of what they might say, and the repercussions they might invoke. But they're angry about water.

Along the stretch from Swan Hill to Mildura a large, foreign-controlled, publicly-listed company has been buying up tracts of land, and using water licences bought on the open market to plant almonds. Thousands of acres of them. I'm told the end product is destined for India.

I've no reason to believe the company is operating outside the law, just as I've no doubt it is legally leveraging the tax breaks the government is offering. But all the locals can see, as their own crops die of thirst, is a big player moving into the market and taking over, with the full support of their own government.

You don't have to be a genius to see that as trouble brewing.

I'm reminded of a conversation I had with one of the many regional water regulators I spoke to on the trip.

'The face of farming is definitely changing,' she told me. 'If you're a little farmer it's really hard to survive. Corporate farming is really taking over and moving away from the small family operation, and it will be a loss to the communities, and a painful transition. But I think we all realise that the farming communities we look at today will not be like that in ten years' time.'

And, just as an aside, I've noticed when citrus or grape growers in this area turn the water off and let a crop die, sometimes they keep watering the plant closest to the road at the head of the row, so you get a living perimeter around a dead orchard. I'm not exactly sure if it's meant to hide or highlight the dead trees behind, but it's a strong statement either way.

I take Benino to the junction of the Murrumbidgee and the Murray to show her where the two great rivers meet, but she's too young to understand its significance. I have an eerie feeling our river's names will become very important to her generation, and not just as hangouts for swagmen and bushrangers romanticised in poetry and song.

There is no flow from the 'Bidgee, except perhaps a little backflow from the Murray. Nonetheless it's a beautiful setting and I would have camped there if I'd been alone, but I know of a better spot for Benino at Boundary Bend.

It's a sandy cay on the inside of a bend in the river, and it's ideal for our purposes because I can get *The Parrot* almost to the river's edge. We cook dinner on an open fire and eat as the sun sets. Benino catches her first Yellowbelly, and then gets her clarinet out and I get the guitar and we jam while the stars fill the sky.

We eat the fish for breakfast and as we're leaving Benino says, 'That was really fun,' which is the biggest rap I've ever heard her give something that doesn't involve a computer or an ice-cream.

'For me too, sweetheart,' I say. 'For me too.'

SMART COWS

I'm starting to entertain some fairly bizarre notions. Like seeing humans as cows, for instance; smart cows, sure, but ultimately lazy, ignorant, methane-producing cows nonetheless. This is a dangerous state of affairs, I know. But it's hard not to when you start trying to make sense of our behaviour.

We hang around in mobs waiting to be fed and watered, and make a big noise if it doesn't happen when we want it to. We make a mess wherever we choose and just turn our backs on it. We're creatures of habit, but still curious enough to walk from one corner of our paddock to the other just to see what's there. And we daren't do anything new unless someone else shows us it's okay, and then we all rush to get to the front of the line to make sure we don't miss out; like the cows in that Gary Larson cartoon going crook when another cow tries to push into the line-up to the abattoirs.

Oh dear. Maybe it's time I went in for a rest, take my tablets, and stop thinking for a spell.

We go down to Wonthaggi to see about the desalination plant the Victorian government is planning as part of their water strategy for Melbournians. The site is pristine coastal real estate, and understandably a couple of landholders about to have their property compulsorily acquired for the plant are strongly opposed.

'It's a very seductive solution, to take water from the ocean, take the salt out of it, and pump it to Melbourne,' one of the landholders says. 'And while it's being portrayed as that simple, people don't need to pay attention to anything else. It's just a convenient solution that doesn't touch any of the end users, be they commercial or to a lesser extent householders; there's no incentive to change there. Every time the governments find another silver bullet remedy, like this one, or the north–south pipeline from the Murray, people living in the city think it's business as usual.'

'So how do you change people's thinking in the cities?' I ask.

'Well,' says her partner, 'I think if we knew how to do that we'd do it, because if we build this plant here, people in Melbourne are going to continue using water for the next twenty years the same as they did in the past twenty years. And that's what's got to change.'

Tellingly, while I'm getting some vox pops to gauge the opinion of locals on the streets of Wonthaggi, opinion is divided and awareness is high, with the exception of one young couple:

'Are you locals?'

'No, we're holidaying.'

'No matter. What do you think of the idea of a desalination plant here in Wonthaggi?'

'Is there?'

'Sure is. Where are you from?'

'Melbourne.'

'Well it's actually for your water.'

'Is it?' she says. 'I love water.'

'Seems we're all quite fond of it,' I say, laughing.

'Well,' he says, 'I used to be a dairy farmer and I'm used to using recycled water, so I can't see a problem with it.'

I find it telling that his response focuses on the quality of the water, rather than the viability of the method of supply. And at that moment it's hard for me to shake the image of those two young people as cows bent over the water trough back in Melbourne, sucking in the big ones, completely unconcerned and unaware of its origins.

UNFORGETTABLE

You don't often meet a natural-born storyteller. And, unless you're in the right frame of mind, it's easy to pass one by. This one I come across while I'm chasing leads to a different story. She's tending a surf shop for a friend, and she has her daughter with her at the time so I ask her name.

'My daughter's name is Envy,' she tells me.

'As in one of the seven deadly sins?'

'Yes, that's it. But that's not quite how it came about.'

At this point I decide to drop my earlier story and talk to her instead. She looks a cruisy style of a woman with a little touch of hippy and dollop of cool, but there's something about the way she left the door open that makes me think she has a story. I tell her to hold that thought and go to fetch the microphone. When I return she is straightening clothes.

'So, how did it come about?'

'Envy's name? I had a bad reaction to the morphine during my caesarean section and I went strange for about sixteen hours. Everyone said I was fine, but I don't remember any of it. Anyway, in that time the family all wanted to know what her name was going to be, the first granddaughter on both sides, and when I came to, there was the name Envy Troy written on the card in my handwriting.'

'And there was no background at all, no previous reference?'

'No, none at all. We had all these lovely old-fashioned names picked out, but when I came back to earth, there it was written on her cradle: Envy Troy.'

'What did your husband say at the time?'

'He knew better than to argue, so he didn't say anything. But I did say to him when I came around, 'What the hell were you thinking?''

'And again he said nothing, right?'

'Yeah, like I said, he knows better.'

'So what names did you have on the list?'

'My partner wanted Ivy. And I wanted Aria. While I was pregnant I was watching the Aria awards on television, and I liked the name. Envy was never on any list.'

She continues realigning clothes on their hangers as she speaks, occasionally looking up at me with a grin to highlight an absurdity, but mostly she just chats away while she works and needs very little prompting.

'And the scariest thing was, when she was born she was eight pound eight, but she was fifty-seven centimetres long, and she had the longest fingers and the longest toes of any baby that I'd ever seen.

'And of course I woke up and all I saw were the capital letters ET, for Envy Troy, and these long, dangly fingers.'

'ET phone home.'

'That's right. And my sister and I ended up having babies on the same day in the same hospital, so we were in opposite beds with these newborn babies born three hours apart, and she reckons all she could hear was me shaking my head and saying, 'But she's such a funny-looking baby.'

'And we had to strip them down to give them their first baths, and I kept cutting myself to the back of the line because I didn't want to strip her down in front of the others because she took up the whole length of the bath. And there were all these other babies in there looking as other babies do, and I had Envy!'

'Any more to follow?'

'I hope so. I always wanted eight. I've got a list of names.'

'But you don't work from a list: you shoot from the hip.'

'I know. But they're good names!' and she laughs.

And, for the record, Envy is within earshot for the whole of this conversation and has obviously heard it all before because she makes no outward sign of being affected in any way.

I ask her what she thinks of her name and she just shrugs the way young adolescent girls do and says, 'It's cool.'

No doubt growing up with a mother like hers she's learned to accept the fact that everything's fair game when it comes to storytelling, and there's a stronger than average probability she'll grow up with a keen sense of humour herself. That, and the unforgettable name, should pretty much guarantee her a noteworthy passage.

BELLWETHER PROFILE

A bellwether is a sheep with a natural tendency to lead, a trait the farmer uses by hanging a bell around his neck so the rest of the flock know when its time to move on.

If you're of the opinion sheep have no brains then it might seem a risky thing to leave the flock to the mercy of one of its own. But a mate of mine who grew up with sheep believes they're not so much stupid, as confused. They just want to do sheep things, and we're forever asking them to follow human logic. It's true that left to its own devices in a suitable environment a flock of sheep will generally keep itself fed, watered and sheltered, and individually each and every adult sheep in the flock will know what it needs.

To a lesser or greater degree the same is true of an electorate of people, albeit with needs slightly (but only slightly – remember the cows) more complex. Nearly every individual knows what it needs, and collectively the flock will decide what's best for the majority.

We call it democracy and, while it's not rocket science, it is very exacting. Assuming a level playing field for the contest, a population will always get precisely what it believes it needs, and it will always be right.

Of course, time may prove its choice to be something other than it imagined or was led to believe, or circumstances may change either its needs or its beliefs or both, but essentially democracy works.

They call Eden–Monaro the bellwether electorate because when it changes the country follows. Consequently the electorate is closely scrutinised every election by journalists and political parties alike, and you'll hear terms like litmus seat, diversity, and representative demographics bandied about ad nauseam.

The likely reason it's such a good indicator of the national voting trend is because the mix of human activity – vocational, recreational, fiscal, social, environmental and so on – is so varied and proportionately distributed it presents a fair approximation of the mix nationwide.

One of the recreational activities the area is famous for is motorbike riding, and, thanks to its location about midway between Sydney and Melbourne and the bike-friendly roads in the vicinity, the southern Eden–Monaro town of Bombala has become something of a bikers' mecca.

Indeed, it's grown so popular as a bikers' stopover that many of the town's small businesses have come to rely on their custom, and one man I meet has even opened up a bed and breakfast especially catering for bikers.

Coincidentally, Bombala's yearly bikers' bash is being held on election weekend so I ask him how bikers vote.

'Look I don't know,' he says. 'These days motorcyclists come from all walks of life. Yes, they might all wear leather, and it might be black leather. And yes they might have a beard. But the leather's there to protect them if they fall off. And the beard's there to protect their teeth from the flies when they're smiling.

'But certainly I've noticed a marked change in the Eden–Monaro region, living here.

'When I first moved here it was staunchly Liberal, but due to a lot of factors such as health and education and employment – it's alright saying the country's got low unemployment, but this area hasn't – and I think it's a matter of social justice, and it's a shame and a legacy of the Howard government that we have become a nation who doesn't see matters of social justice as important as we used to.'

At about this point he tells me he's just lost his wife to cancer, and the anger in his voice comes forward in the mix.

'And the health care in this region – Tony Abbott was on the television the other day saying the longest wait anyone could expect for medical services in this country was four hours.

'Well I can tell you now if you were to wait only four hours there'd be no problem. Eight weeks is a good wait to see a GP in this town.

'So it's absolute rubbish. It may be that in the city that's the case, but towns like this are the backbone of this country; they are historically branded on the psyche of Australians thanks to Banjo Patterson and poets like him, as what Australia is all about.

'Well, it's not easy to live here, it's certainly not easy to get a job, it's ridiculously difficult to see a doctor, and something needs to happen. Seriously.'

Is that the distant ringing of a bell I hear?

Note: For the record, the vox pops I took in the Eden-Monaro in as many towns as I had time to visit in three days, indicated the bell was ringing loudly.

HOUND DOG

I have a journalist mate fresh back from Nashville. He's living with his brother in Port Lonsdale, the first town west of Port Phillip Bay on the Bass Strait coast.

We have history, this mate and I. But it's been almost twenty years since we saw each other and we've both changed. He is a thin man now, where he once was round. His face carries too much skin and the folds barely hide the cracks. He reminds me of a basset hound.

He is also quieter than I remember him, more circumspect. Still bright, but without the crackle and fizz he used to have. Is that what we lose first, what spills from our pockets while we're not looking?

He says it's because the quiet hound is the real deal, while the old hound was another dog he was trying out at the time. He could be right: most of us work out who we are by eliminating who we aren't.

The kernel remains, though, whatever the shell. He still knows things, and he's still learning. When I first knew him, he knew two things about the world. Now he knows three.

His latest acquisition is golf – picked up because he's been covering the US golf tour for the last few seasons – and his playing partner at the moment is the family dog: an effervescent young thing as powerless to resist chasing balls as my friend is to resist hitting them. And they make a good couple: the coiled spring of a kelpie pup and the tired old basset hound with the errant obsessive-compulsive gene.

The next and most interesting thing he knows is almost every possible travel itinerary to and from every major city in the world. Ask him how to get from Beijing to Lima and he'll give you three options without pausing. He knows this stuff because he's fascinated by travel, by the possibilities of travel, and I believe because he is never settled in himself and this is his vicarious escape.

The last thing he knows is politics. He knows politics like only an old journalist can know politics. They don't take sides when it comes to politics; for a journalist everyone is fair game and the hunting's best at election time. And he loves the post-mortem because, he says, it's the only time politicians ever give you the truth.

We stay the night and catch up. The talk is music, golf, politics, the country – though mostly music and golf. Back in Nashville he has befriended one of Bob Dylan's band members and has been trying to line up a round of golf with Bob, who's apparently just taken it up with a vengeance as well.

My mate is undecided about going back to work in the US: he loves the opportunities it offers but the cynic in him finds it soulless at times. He is, after all, a journalist.

And we're going to Tasmania. Benino's been looking forward

to Tassie ever since we began this leg, but not for any reason I would have thought.

It's not the opportunity to spend time with her nanna, who my sister believes should make a perfect playmate for her since they're now at about the same level of maturity. Nor is it the novelty of having a sleeping cabin for the ferry trip, with its own porthole through which we may see whales or dolphins or fantastical marine creatures of her imagination.

No, my daughter is excited about going to Tasmania because she knows they have a buffet on board the ferry, and she thinks buffets are about the greatest development in food since the invention of chocolate.

'What's so special about buffets?' I ask her.

'They're really cool,' she sets me straight. Then she launches into an impromptu rendition of her *dance of great happiness*, complete with cheer girl finger pointing and various semi-choreographed moves she's picked up watching music clips and other irresistible cultural indicators. Like I said, she's looking forward to the buffet.

I've been looking forward to the Tassie leg with mixed feelings. On the one hand it marks the beginning of the last week of the trip before I take a break, a milestone I'm relieved to be reaching.

The flip side is it also marks the beginning of the last week with my daughter. Time is a thief in a harlequin suit.

I ask my friendly basset hound what time the *Spirit of Tasmania* leaves and of course he knows off the cuff.

The last thing he tells me is not to worry, there will be a change of government. And it's the first time I realise how much I am worried, and how much, after travelling the country for much of the year, I feel it needs the change almost as much as it needs the rain.

CHANGE WITH
A GREEN TINGE

Nobody takes Tasmania seriously. Somehow she gets left off national maps, foreign tourists think she is a different country, and mainlanders and Taswegians alike perpetuate the myth (?) of inbreeding.

Yet of all Australia's states she is arguably the one we should take the most seriously, since all that is good and bad about European settlement in Australia is clearly manifest in Tasmania's past and present.

On the negative side of the ledger you'll find our most shocking case of genocide (Tasmanian Aborigines), our bloodiest contemporary massacre (Port Arthur), our most visible extinction (the Thylacine), and one of our grossest acts of environmental negligence (Queenstown), among others I'm sure you could tell me.

And on the positive side she has maintained some of the world's most pristine wilderness and magnificent old-growth forests, astounding levels of biodiversity, including an enviable array of flora and fauna endemic to the island, waters still teeming with aquatica and soil rich enough to sustain all manner of agriculture, and all this in an underpopulated state of a developed first-world country.

Tasmania could easily become the place to be when climate change starts getting nasty. Only problem with that plan, of course, is once two or three million people clamber onto the island to stake their claim in paradise, all that is unique and beautiful about her now will be long gone.

The trip across Bass Strait is uneventful and (once the buffet experience has been fully explored, of course) Benino and I sleep right through till the purser's imminent arrival announcement blows us out of bed. The Captain tells me the weather's been kind of late, and the most interesting event on the way over was one of the fishermen in Port Phillip Bay holding up a monster snapper he'd just caught as the ship passed.

He says they also see the occasional squid boat on the crossing, with lights ablaze to attract the squid, and sometimes whales and dolphins, the latter only able to keep up with the ship's twenty-seven-knot cruising speed for short spells.

'Otherwise,' he says, 'it's steady as she goes.'

Once processed by an overly officious quarantine official (all is forgiven: I'll never criticise the happy ones again) Benino and I head for Launceston. It's election day and we'll be spending the business end of the vote counting at a party at one of the local member's offices.

Unfortunately for the party (and the Party) it is at the sitting Liberal member's offices, and there's no sadder place to be on an election night than in losers' headquarters. Heartfelt expressions of disbelief and dismay meet every polling station update as a general feeling of malaise gradually suffocates the room.

The one bright spot for me is when Benino decides that since this is an election party this must also be the right time to wear her Kevin in '07 Labor campaign T-shirt, so she slips out to *The Parrot* and puts it on without my knowledge. Seeing her saunter into that sad old room wearing enemy colours and a winner's grin, completely unaware of the impact she's having, is something to savour for all time.

Of course the result of that election is now history,* but it was the first time in my life I'd followed a federal election closely and had a real handle on the issues, and I was amazed at just how clearly the democratic process can speak when it chooses to. Distilling all I had heard from the country during my trip around, a change with a green tinge was what it told me it needed, and that's exactly what it delivered. It was a result that gave me hope.

The next morning, those of us on opposite sides of the political fence the night before came together for a good-natured post-mortem over breakfast, and there was never a better example of what a great country we live in.

* The John Howard-led Coalition was soundly beaten by Kevin Rudd's Labor Party.

EPILOGUE

By the time the 2020 Summit came around I'd already returned *The Parrot* and taken myself off the road. This meant I was probably the only person attending without a job, a fixed address or an area of expertise. It made for some enigmatic introductions.

The show was kicked off in fine style in the Great Hall of Parliament House with a bit of a tune on the didgeridoo, all stand for the National Anthem, and a welcoming speech from one of the traditional owners of the land, which she began beautifully with, 'Am I supposed to say youse can all sit?'

Then after the remaining formalities, including a pep talk from the PM, we were herded off into our respective streams for briefings by our co-chairs and appropriate ministers, before being further divided into four 'sub-streams' to begin the process of 'shaking the fruit from the trees', or gathering all our great ideas to ensure Australia reached 2020 in better shape than it was now.

Facilitators then took over and under their instruction all our great big ideas were written on tiny little post-it notes, which cut even the grandest down to size. Then the notes were arranged on the whiteboard using a process I think they called 'silent sorting', whereby we stuck them up and then wordlessly shuffled them around into unlikely groups.

Then came the square peg in the round hole bit, where all the ideas in the newly sorted groups were combined to produce one or two big ideas, by whatever means necessary. Here's where teeth were bared and tempers flared, and the more functional groups compromised and produced something worth presenting to the main group when we reassembled later that afternoon.

The next step proved the contentious one, where all the ideas from the mighty to the meek went to the PM's office for overnight perusal, before coming back to us the next morning in what some saw as greatly altered condition. There were even accusations of ideas surfacing on the Sunday that weren't authored on the

Saturday – the much-publicised HECS-repayment-in-skill scheme for students, to name one example – but, while I noticed a few inconsistencies, I couldn't say there were any sexy ideas planted in our stream (for surely they'd have been conspicuous by their very presence). I will say, though, it would have been almost impossible for anyone to keep track of all the ideas tabled on the Saturday, particularly those that didn't survive the first round. So if the government scrutineers did, as they promised, consider every idea voiced, it's entirely possible they could have picked up the germ of an idea from the scrap heap and given it new life.

Curiously, the idea I remember with the most clarity was the grandiose 'We are the key' address by the only genuine fringe dweller in our midst. He rejected the group process entirely and delivered his unadulterated message from the lectern like a preacher to his flock, beseeching us all to do something (not sure exactly what he had in mind) while we still could. His good intentions were noted as surely as his judgement was flawed; as one friend said to me afterwards, 'I was happy to go with him till he started talking about making love: I'm sorry, but sex and Parliament House just doesn't work for me.' Later on he conducted a sit-in on the stage in the Great Hall – his purple lanyard clearly identifying him as one of our (the rural stream's) finest – and it was fascinating to watch security having to deal with the problem tactfully under the benevolent gaze of a thousand summiteers (not forgetting the posse of news cameras).

But, diversions aside, the only contribution I could see that my group had made was a phrase from our mission statement that somehow freed itself from the idea we lumbered it with on the Saturday, and resurfaced with another idea on the Sunday morning after a sleepover in the PM's office. It was hardly a defining moment in the history of Australian policy-making.

I did do some external lobbying for more demerit points on drivers' licences, on the grounds that a dozen isn't nearly enough for a country of this size and watching out for ever-varying speed limits turns good drivers into nervous wrecks; but it's hard to get people to take you seriously these days.

The catering was kept basic, to avoid 'taxpayer-funded talkfest' criticism, and there was something bizarre about standing among heads of industry, small-business owners, farmers and senior academics making big talk over little lunch packs. I guess if you were the sort of person who enjoyed the whole schoolyard politics thing it would have felt comforting; I found it a bit like a barbeque without booze.

But was the Summit a worthwhile exercise? I think yes. Sure there were cynics and yes it seemed to be agenda-driven (by participants certainly, and government probably), but so what? For a brief period and for the first time I can remember, we had most of the population – not just Summit delegates – seriously considering what would make Australia a better place. That alone can't be a bad thing, whatever else did, didn't, will or won't result.

And did I contribute anything worthwhile? Highly unlikely. It takes a level of political skill I simply don't possess to make a difference in that sort of environment, and it was naive of me to think people wanted to be reacquainted with the elephant in the corner of the room. The abolition of state governments in favour of bolstered local government precincts – in other words, two tiers of government – has been mooted many times over the last hundred years, and each time it gets put back in the too-hard basket because of the majority-of-a-majority clause in the constitution.* As one of my fellow summiteers said to me, 'We're English; we don't do revolution. We make changes slowly.'

Even so, it looks obvious to me that something has to be done, and I'm not convinced we have that much time to act. Even with Labor holding every office in the country we can't even take the baby step of banning plastic bags! What's going to happen when we have to start making the real lifestyle sacrifices?

Of course, on the surface at least, this is more a governance than a rural issue, but if I may use water as both a recent case in point and an ongoing metaphor for many problems in the bush, if you follow it upstream far enough you'll likely come to a problem at state level. I'm not saying the states have a mortgage on mismanagement, merely that we can't afford so many layers of it and states are the obvious evictees.

But it's probably political suicide, and in any case I couldn't even get it past the parochial defence of my sub-group. Happily, the more achievable 'harmonisation of standards across the states' got up as our best and fairest idea, and some would say it went on to become one of the most influential players of the Summit, as the call for a more federal approach to problem-solving was articulated in many of the streams. (Another strong performer was the push for a republic, which came from the floor, despite accusations to the contrary, and which, like better or non-existent state governance, I believe we must embrace sooner or later.)

So that was the Australian 2020 Summit for me. Not entirely a waste of time because I met some fine people and had a chance to cross-check a few points raised in this book. But as for thinking I could make a real contribution to the heady world of policy-making just because I'd done a lap of the country talking to people, I've decided I'm better off staying in my own world and making my contributions from the heart.

* Would require a referendum to be passed by a majority of people in a majority of states.

ABOUT THE AUTHOR

Monte Dwyer is best known in Australia for his time as a roving weatherman on a popular breakfast television show, a role he held long enough to need therapy. He is also a qualified nurse, a trained performer, a produced playwright, a keen musician and an all-round media journeyman. When he is not on the road he lives in Sydney and complains about the cost of living.